THE LONG HAUL

THE LONG HAUL

TRUCKERS, TRUCK STOPS & TRUCKING

by
JAMES H. THOMAS

Memphis State University Press
Memphis State University

Contents

For Johnna, Julie, and Jason

Preface

The trucker has a position unique in American history and mythology. Simultaneously he serves as a vital link between the people of the nation and the goods they desire, and as a folk hero. In fact, he occupies the same niche filled in the 19th century by cowboys, railroad engineers, and stagecoach drivers and in previous centuries by the sailor. He is regarded as worldly, mechanically knowledgeable, physically strong, and attractive to the opposite sex. In short, he is the hero of ballads, the idol of youngsters, a "knight of the road." This study is an attempt to trace the history of this industry and to explain how truckers earned their romantic image.

Recently there have been several studies, both popular and scholarly, about truckers and trucking. However, this work is unique in that it seeks the thread connecting myth and reality. The methodology is simple. By tracing the industry from its birth to maturity, including major technological advancements, the basis is laid for an examination of the trucker's role in American life and a discussion of the myth surrounding those who drive the big "rigs." Although many of the tales concerning these rugged individuals emphasize the masculine character of the driver, this study concludes that the stereotype rapidly is fading because of technological advances. Today's driver no longer, of necessity, comes from the lower end of the economy or the rougher elements of society. Automatic transmissions, citizens' band radios, mobile mechanics, and tire repair service available anywhere make it possible for the driver to be mechanically illiterate and physically weak—or female.

The future of the industry is uncertain, for new advances come almost weekly.

During this investigation I incurred numerous debts, which I here acknowledge. For his constant interest and helpful suggestions, his friendship and advice, his loan of materials, his proofreading and editing, and for his encouragement, I owe a great debt to Dr. Carl N. Tyson. I would also like to thank my brother-trucker, Hugh, for his intelligent answers to my foolish questions. Furthermore, I appreciate Geri Becker Schott, Catherine Porter, and Gale Petry for typing the manuscript and remaining in good humor through all of my editorial changes. Moreover, I acknowledge the Wichita State University's Research Committee whose support helped me complete this project.

February 1, 1979
JAMES H. THOMAS
Wichita, Kansas

The "Knight of the Road"

From the moment colonization began in what would come to be the United States, Americans have been a people on the move—rootless, restless, expansive. The great migration westward, by wagon train, stagecoach, steamboat, or railroad, produced a class of men seen in the popular mind as heroic—if somewhat crude. These people, the wagon master, stagecoach driver, steamboat captain, and railroad engineer, were helping America achieve its destiny as they traversed unknown lands and scattered pioneers and goods across the untamed wilderness. The cracking of a bull-whip, the shrill whistle of a steamboat, and the hiss of escaping steam from a locomotive announced that communication and transportation with the great outside world were at hand.

The arrival of these cargo carriers in isolated communities often was the most exciting event of the day, week, or even month. News of the outside world could be had, scarce merchandise could be purchased, and tales of exotic places could be heard. As the transportation network improved, farm commodities could be shipped to outside markets, and both necessities and frivolous luxuries could be purchased. Little wonder that those who commanded these vehicles should become heroes to people living in isolation; not only did the bull whacker, stage driver, or engineer provide needed freight and markets, but also he could tell wondrous tales of distant places and events. There was an aura of romance to such men, for they were seen as worldly, independent, and masculine; yet, simultaneously, they were somewhat unsavory, for they lacked the stability and steadfastness of ordinary mortals.

This dependence on common carriers gradually ended with the adoption of the horseless carriage. As automobiles became more commonplace and as roads were improved, the farmer could escape his isolation and see the city lights, while the urban dweller could flee the crowded city for jaunts into the countryside. Increasingly the automobile became the national symbol of the United States; a country whose heritage was individual mobility would have an enduring love affair with the automobile. In fact, few objects in world history have received the attention and worship that Americans have lavished on their cars, for this gave them something they highly prized: freedom of travel.

At first the rich enjoyed their cars for pleasure and prestige. Then, as production increased, the middle-class urban dweller could afford a used car or even a new but inexpensive model. At last Henry Ford produced his Model T, the "Tin Lizzie," in such incredible numbers and at such a low price that blue-collar workers and farmers could afford them.

The automobile wrought a social revolution in the United States. Country towns began to wither away, for rural dwellers could drive in their cars to larger towns to shop. Young people could do their courting with greater privacy—and such anonymity that some moralists called the automobile "a bedroom on wheels." Cultural events were available to far greater audiences, and provincialism declined in direct proportion to the spread of the automobile.

At the same time that the automobile was changing the face of America, the technology behind this contrivance was making possible yet another revolution: the trucking industry. No longer did goods and commodities have to move by railroad. Trucks were not confined to narrow ribbons of steel, and truckers could serve both city and countryside with transportation services. The trucker did not halt his vehicle at the end of paved road, but extended his routes over impossible dirt tracks. And once again, the public imagination had found a romantic hero. Here was a breed of men conquering a wilderness, fighting machines, bad roads, and the elements. At each sleepy hamlet, small boys were awestruck at the sight of large, sputtering, smoking trucks. While their fathers asked questions about the mechanical aspects of the vehicle or else circled it to kick the tires, the boys looked at the driver and dreamed of the day when they could be in command of such a mechanical monster. The independent trucker did little to puncture the dreams either of fathers, who thought them mechanical geniuses, or of boys, who thought them "knights of the road." In fact, these early-day truckers, like the cowboy before them, came to believe the myths about themselves.

Many of the young lads who worshipped the truckers soon realized their dream. Two major wars brought a growing demand for civilian and military drivers. Moreover, the conditions of wartime were in many ways similar to those encountered by pioneer truckers: wrestling vehicles across difficult terrain under impossible schedules. And in both cases the drivers resisted societal and organizational restraints; in fact, personnel in the Army's Motor Corps considered themselves truckers first and soldiers second. Then, at the end of each war, veterans returned home to utilize their recently learned occupation—and they yearned to display the independence which Army life had denied them. Orders, rules, and regulations, they felt, had robbed them of their personal freedom, and they yearned for the life of a trucker, which seemed to promise unlimited opportunity and independence for a young, hard-working entrepreneur willing to live on the road.

The myths presently held about trucks and truckers evolved from the practices of independent truckers in the period following the end of World War I. At that time truckers had the image of being totally free. The actual driving of a truck required few skills beyond those of the average motorist, but in those days the trucker needed physical strength to change tires and mechanical knowledge to make repairs. Theirs was a demanding, semi-nomadic experience which set them apart.

By the middle of the depression, interstate trucking had become big business, and by the end of World War II the breed had marked characteristics which set them apart from other travelers. Even the most unsophisticated traveler, walking into a highway cafe, would recognize the man humped over a cup of coffee, enshrouded in cigarette smoke, as the driver of the large truck

The Army Motor Corps constructing a roadbed near the Mexican Border during the Pancho Villa campaign. *Courtesy White Motor Corporation.*

parked outside. His unpressed clothes, uncombed hair, and perhaps the tattoo on his forearm set him apart from the tourist. The image of the trucker would remain fairly constant until the mid to late 1960s. On the socioeconomic scale, the trucker would remain near the bottom—if a somewhat romantic figure.[1]

One of the most pervasive images of the trucker is that he is part outlaw, defying almost everything from Interstate Commerce Commission regulations and speed limits to maximum weight laws. Although the trucker's independent nature prevents total stereotyping, some generalizations are possible. Most often each trucker operates within a rigid social framework based on his relationship with the commodities he carries and the system in which he receives his pay. At the top of the social scale is the owner-operator with the most expensive and powerful rig, receiving payment on cargo based on a percentage of freight revenues. At the bottom of the scale is the regional hauler of agricultural products, operating an outdated company truck and drawing an hourly rate. The topics of conversation among truckers center around the machine; destination is of secondary importance except during the winter months when road conditions are discussed.

The trucker, seemingly unaffected by the vast cultural differences encountered on his travels, possesses traits associated with the South or Midwest. His attitudes, dress, and speech patterns are a mixture of the two regions and may be attributed to the large percentage of truckers with rural backgrounds and an interest in country and western music. Truckers from the Northeast or Northwest who engage in the long-haul soon lose their regional, cultural traits and come to resemble their counterparts who hail from Oklahoma or Mississippi. This rich mixture of Southern and Midwestern culture, often associated with the cowboy of the nineteenth century, compels writers to compare the modern trucker with the cowhand.[2] The myths, symbols, and legends attached to both occupations becloud cultural definitions and objective comparisons. Nevertheless, both cowboy and trucker reflect the ceaseless wandering of a highly mobile society. The daily drudgery of both occupations is lost amidst descriptions of the adventures encountered on journeys up the dusty Chisholm Trail or its modern concrete equivalent, Interstate 35.

Independent trucker Chuck "Double Deuce" Cannan drives his Mack out of California. *From the author's collection.*

Trucker heading up the dusty trail into the setting sun. *Courtesy International Trucks.*

Heroes, myths, and symbols come from those traits the general population holds in high esteem, or those which allow the public to live their most treasured fantasies vicariously. The outstanding characteristics of both the cowboy and the trucker are independence, mobility, power, courage, and masculinity. The myth dictates that members of both occupations enjoy complete freedom, and that when conditions of employment are unbearable they ride/drive into the sunset. Thus the trucker and cowboy have an independence not enjoyed—but sought—by most members of American society. Mobility, the great American pastime, reflects the national feeling that moving to a different region brings happiness and prosperity; such is the foundation of a public awe for the

The noble steed of the modern cowboy. *Courtesy Marsha Holmberg.*

transporters of goods. The Appaloosa stallion and the six-gun were symbols of power for the cowboy; in more recent times, a diesel-powered Kenworth is the trucker's steed, and command of a 60,000-pound cargo wrapped in chrome and steel is the trucker's power symbol. Courage is necessary to control such awesome power to turn a stampeding herd or to ride to the bottom of a mountain road when the brakes fail. Masculinity is the principal ingredient that unifies these heroic traits. Therefore women connected to both occupations have played the role of ever-waiting spouses or girl friends, or employees at their cultural centers: the saloon at the end of the trail and the pro-am truckstop beside the interstate highway.

The mystique that surrounds the trucker, unlike that of the cowboy, has not been utilized to any large degree by the popular media as a central theme until quite recently. Whereas the Western became a major theme of movies almost from the birth of that industry, trucking and drivers were featured only in a few cases. Humphrey Bogart's portrayal of a trucker in the movie, "They Drive by Night," did not produce a new genre, only a few grade "B" films. However, beginning in the 1970s trucking has been discovered as a subject matter for made-for-television films and even a couple of series. "Duel," starring Dennis Weaver (who usually was associated with cowboy roles), started a trend. In this less-than-epic show, the truck symbolized the power of a machine and the helplessness of an individual caught in the wake of a mindless bulk of nuts and bolts. The driver of the truck, hidden behind a dusty and tinted windshield, was never shown to the audience as he tried to kill Weaver, the hapless driver of an automobile.

Other recent films include "White Line Fever," starring Jan-Michael Vincent, which follows the stereotype of the independent trucker fighting the corporations and depicts the hero as moral, masculine, and independent;"Convoy," which is based on the song of the same name and romanticizes the trucker; "Smokey and the Bandit," with Burt Reynolds and Sally Fields, in which the hero bets he can drive from Georgia to Texarkana to pick up a load of Coors beer and return within 40 hours; "Citizens Band," which depicts the wide use of CB's after the energy crunch of 1973; and "The Steel Cowboys," which portrays the plight of an independent trucker forced to move rustled steers in order to make the payments on his truck. Several other films have appeared, but none of them has been so successful at the box office or in the Nielsen ratings as to make them especially noteworthy.

Television has contributed to the development of the modern image of the trucker by its news coverage of the Teamsters Union and the independent truckers' strikes, and by a few attempts at investigative reporting. The weekly television news program "Sixty Minutes" produced a segment devoted to the life of the trucker. However, time limitations, selection of the individual, and insufficient study on the subject resulted in a glossing over of only a few of the cultural elements of trucking. The follow-up of the "Sixty

Minutes" segment on the "Tomorrow Show" gave more indepth coverage, but again fell short of producing a documentary on truckers. Tom Snyder, the host of "Tomorrow," sought the unusual and sensational, and at the same time he appeared ill-informed on many aspects of trucking. The weekly television series "Moving On" did not closely resemble the life of an owner-operator, but the truck gave the producers of the show a mobile medium through which unique situations could be presented, while a series projected for the spring of 1979 featuring two female teamsters promises to be a bit of fluffy nonsense.

Popular magazines, such as *Reader's Digest, Saturday Evening Post,* and *Esquire,* have published articles on trucking, but these have merely touched the surface; a journalist reported his experiences while riding with one trucker on one long haul. Books of the subject are limited in scope and number. *Motor Wagons,* a work compiled by the Pioneer Motor Club of America, did not analyze the role of the trucker; rather it provided some interesting anecdotes from the 1930s. The only attempt to date to analyze trucking as a micro-culture is Jane Stern's *Trucker: A Portrait of the Last American Cowboy.* The author presented many interesting and unusual stories about truckers, but received poor reviews from truckers' magazines for dwelling on women truckers and the promiscuous sexual activities of drivers. However, at the date of its publication, Stern's work not only was the first book that approached the subject from the point of view of popular culture, but also was a readable and informative work on an almost unexplored subject.

Truckers are not without a voice in the popular media. The single largest factor in popularizing trucking culture came with the adoption of the citizens' band (CB) radio in trucks and automobiles. CB's had become a part of the trucking industry, but did not have wide use until the independent truckers' strike of 1973. After national coverage of the strikers' use of the radio, the demand for CB's became insatiable. Not only did the general population want to listen in on truckers' conversations, but also to take part in exchanging information about road conditions and the whereabouts of state police. The fad that surrounded the CB radio in the mid-1970s produced another important statement about the trucking culture, this time from country and western music. When C. W.

McCall's "Convoy" topped the record charts, many country music fans purchased CB's. The story of the song involved a group of truckers who were able to avoid speeding tickets by the use of radio communication. The first truck, called the front door, could report any police radar units or highway patrol cars, and the last truck in the convoy, or back door, was responsible for the same, making trucks in the middle immune to detection. The second most important record of this genre was "White Knight." In it a highway patrolman with a CB lured a trucker into speeding by impersonating a trucker protecting the back door.[3]

By 1978 the trucker has come to symbolize an independent spirit. He reflects mobility, power, and anti-establishment values—with a slight tinge of illegal activities to add the spice needed to create an American hero. As with legendary figures of the past, however, the trucker's image is more myth than fact. The modern trucker does not see himself as heir to the wagon master, stagedriver, sailor, or locomotive engineer. Nor does he, for the most part, feel any kinship with those pioneer mechanics and drivers who developed the machines of today.

Where now there are dozens of lights, gauges, and toggle switches, there once were two gauges and a starter button, and before that a crank and a lever or two. Where once it took physical brawn and some mechanical knowledge, along with iron kidneys and clenched teeth, to wrestle a truck even a hundred miles, the trucker today has hydraulic cushions to soothe his back, cool air flows to chill him whatever the weather outside, and music from a stereo radio or eight-track tape player to fill his cab. From New York to Chicago in 15 hours, from Dallas to Los Angeles in 30 hours, the trucking man rushes to move the next load, encased in his armored home. The modern driver is blessed with almost any comfort he can imagine, including television, leather paneling, and a foam mattress in his sleeper. But his modern truck and its richness, along with the road over which he drives, did not spring forth from some driver's dreams. These were the result of hard years of work and technological advances, while the creation of the myth about trucking sprang from some deep need in the American consciousness.

Early Trucks and Trucking

Before there were trucks there were automobiles. As early as the 1830s, self-propelled carriages moved on the roads of England. These, like many of the early "cars," were powered by steam boilers which required inordinate amounts of fuel and water, and they had an unsettling tendency to explode. Because of public misgivings about these self-propelled vehicles, such as the assertion that humans could not survive at the rapid speed of 30 miles per hour because the wind would prevent breathing, these early attempts to provide over-the-road transportation were soon legislated out of existence. However, progress could not be deterred. If steam was unreliable and dangerous, inventors would find something better. In 1884 Gottlieb Daimler patented the internal combustion engine fired by gasoline (or petroleum spirits). This new form of power soon was applied to boats, bicycles, and stationary equipment, and by 1887 the French firm of Panhard and Levassor had produced the first workable gasoline-powered automobile. By 1890 the world seemed about to be overwhelmed with these new inventions, as almost every mechanically inclined individual combined the gasoline engine and a three- or four-wheeled carriage to produce his own interpretation of what the automobile should be.[1]

Despite the proliferation of self-powered cars, there was work to be done. Much of this burden fell on Carl Benz and Gottlieb Daimler, two inventive Germans who lived less than 100 miles from one another. Although they pioneered the gasoline-driven automobile and shared geographic proximity, the two leaders reportedly never met. However, their work closely corresponded. Startling new advances were frequently made by each without the other's knowledge. By the time these two finished, much of the basic machinery of the modern automobile had been created.[2]

Although Daimler and Benz were the pioneers, ingenious Yankees in America soon came to the fore in automotive engineering. Late in 1893, Charles E. and J. Frank Duryea combined a one-cylinder engine with a second-hand carriage to produce the first successful gasoline-powered vehicle in America. Quickly other Americans entered the race. In 1896, the Langert Company of Philadelphia created a gasoline delivery wagon, one of the first trucks to appear on the scene, and entered it in the Cosmopolitan Race (from New York to Irvington-on-the-Hudson and return). Soon Cruickshank Engineering Works of Providence, Rhode Island, Charles E. Woods of Chicago, C. S. Fairchild of Portland, Oregon, and Alexander Winton of Cleveland were competing with the Duryea brothers for dominance in the new industry.[3]

Although gasoline was the most popular form of power, others clung to steam. The two most successful were the Stanley brothers of Newton, Massachusetts, and the White Sewing Machine Company of Cleveland. Electricity also was a source of propulsion. In 1898, A. L. Riker, an enterprising young graduate of Columbia Law School, entered a battery-powered wagon in an electrical show held in Madison Square Garden. The most impressive aspect of Riker's wagon was the battery, which weighed more than 1,000 pounds.[4]

Riker's invention, paralleled by the work of Alexander Winton, was of seminal importance because it marked an early excursion into the motor-driven transport of freight. This was a major departure from previous efforts. Whereas the automobile was to most people either an exotic toy or a hobby, the truck was decidedly business-like. Its design and purpose were economic. Although both the car and truck would become necessities, they would take separate routes to acceptance.[5]

The "commercial car," or motor truck, was born from what was considered high luxury in the first decade of the 20th century. The horseless carriage represented "an occular demonstration of

In 1909 Bill Johnson drove the first moving van in California. *Courtesy the Bekins Company.*

the lure of the city, of riches and snobbishness, of unnecessary extravagance and of dust." [6] Local governments passed ordinances banning automobiles from their streets, for these scared the horses and mules used by teamsters hauling freight. However, when second-hand touring automobiles appeared on the market, the trucking industry was born. Merchant and farmer stripped the touring body from the frame, attached a wagon bed to the car skeleton, and the result was a crude but efficient light delivery wagon. As these converted automobiles gained in popularity, there was "a mushroom growth of motor-truck factories." [7]

The infant trucking industry fought hard to overcome the resistance of the general public to a radical change in transportation. Advertisements, manufacturers' shows, and competition between trucks stimulated interest and sales, but increased profits from reducing the cost of moving goods eventually decided the vehicle's future.

Competition between trucks was a direct outgrowth from the established practices of automobile enthusiasts. Automobile touring clubs, by their nature, were competitive. Engineers recorded speed and gas consumption, while drivers tested endurance. The popularity of these contests in the late 1890s, combined with the growth of a manufacturing industry, produced many types of vehicles in various configurations and resulted in the organization of the first formal test for commercial trucks in 1903.

Sponsored by the Automobile Club of America, the event was held in New York City. The stated purpose of the test was to demonstrate to businessmen—and to the public—that commercial truck transportation was not only a possibility but also an economic inevitability. Builders and supporters of trucks previously had asserted that trucks were economically preferable when compared to horse-drawn transportation. This test was to illustrate the truth of this assertion—on a mile-by-mile basis. The event lasted two days and covered 20 miles. The route began at the Automobile Club of America's Club House on Fifth Avenue, circled Central Park to the Battery, and returned to the point of origin.[8]

Eleven companies were represented by 14 entries, demonstrating how rapidly there had been an increase in the number of manufacturers. Because of design specialization, the contest was divided into five divisions. These were assigned according to load capacity. Light delivery wagons were separated into two categories: those carrying less than one ton, and those carrying more than one ton but less than one and one-half tons. Other classifications were less than three tons, less than four tons, and more than four tons. The lightest vehicle entered in the race was a steam-powered truck from the Mobil Company of America. This light wagon used gasoline instead of coal to fire its steam boiler, providing four and one-half horsepower and a load capacity of 750 pounds. The giant of the field was a steam-powered Courtland from Preston, England, which carried 12,000 pounds and boasted 30 horsepower.[9]

Although the 20-mile course could easily be negotiated by to-day's vehicles, it proved a torture test for many of those early trucks. During the first day one of the gasoline-powered wagons failed to finish when a hand pump broke and the fuel caught on fire. The only other casualty was a heavyweight Herschman steam truck with a dry weight of 20,000 pounds. Straining under its load, a 10,000 pound granite brick, it developed a leak in its boiler and was forced to the sidelines. The lighter trucks made two laps around the course in respectable times. The winner, a Waterless Knox, used an eight-horsepower gasoline engine to run the 40-mile course in three hours and 35 minutes; in the process the vehicle used four gallons of gasoline. Among the heavy trucks, a Herschman traveled one and one-half laps in six hours and 30 minutes. The heavy steam truck carried a 3,800 pound load of cobblestones, more than two and one-half times the freight load of the Waterless Knox, but it consumed 230 pounds of coal and 172 gallons of water. The second day of competition was a repeat of the first, except that winners reduced their times for the same run. The light trucks proved their reliability. The Waterless Knox averaged almost eight miles per gallon of gasoline, while an electric entry, the Waverly, used only $2.50 worth of current. However, the English Coulthard needed 1,335 pounds of coke and 869 gallons of water to cover 60 miles. This inefficient vehicle not only was economically unsound, but also its frequent stops to take on fuel and water wasted the most expensive item of transportation cost, labor. Although many were impressed by the race, it clearly did not fulfill its planned objective of gaining general public acceptance for trucks.[10]

The following year the event was repeated. The statistics were more impressive for light trucks, but again the heavy ones appeared too cumbersome to compete with horse-drawn wagons. Unfortunately the trucking industry remained wedded to the technology of early automobiles. Most commercial delivery wagons were made by taking an automobile, stripping off the touring body, and mounting a truck bed on the chassis. Heavier trucks could not be made in this way, however, and their yearly production remained small until World War I.

Truck enthusiasts and builders proved the durability and efficiency of the commercial horseless carriage, but they had to overcome an age-old inclination toward horse-drawn transportation. At first the public demanded that the "devil's wagon" be outlawed from public streets. Trucks caused horses to stampede, roads to erode, and chickens to stop laying. Avid supporters of motor transportation accepted the challenge and fought this prejudice and tradition. An extensive campaign against the horse began. Horseless carriages were reported to be the savior of mankind, the solution to economic ills, the end to an archaic mode of transportation, and the catalyst that would catapult America onto the road to affluence.[11]

Even the basic structure of transportation was questioned. The railroad already had made a tremendous impact on the American economy. Unquestionably the industrial boom between 1865 and 1900 had been aided greatly by the more efficient and less expensive rail transportation. Urban freighting by horse-drawn wagons had not advanced in technology for centuries, while railroads had provided new transportation routes where none had existed. Moreover, the businessman did not have to invest in the railroad, yet from it he received a cheaper or faster service, and the maintenance and operation of freight vehicles were the responsibility of the railroad company.

Trucks offered an extension of the railroads' efficiency—and a replacement for the horse. Popular journals and scientific magazines said "the animal motor" was wasteful, the poorest motor ever built, and an economic anachronism. Yet as late as 1912, most businessmen were hesitant to forsake the estimated $1,000,000,000 investment which they had in 10,000,000 dray horses.[12] The total number of trucks in the United States at the beginning of 1912 was estimated at between 20,000 and 25,000.[13] The increase had been steady, although not spectacular, since the turn of the century. Total truck production in 1913 alone was more than 20,000 vehicles, and by 1917, New York City boasted 25,000 trucks actively engaged in freighting. This increased production and use of the truck illustrated the success of the campaign against "Old Dobbin."[14]

The comparative cost of horse-drawn and truck transportation was overwhelming in favor of the truck. In 1912 a five-ton wagon drawn by three horses could average 45 ton-miles at a cost of eight dollars per day. A motor truck with a five-ton capacity cost twice as

Household moving before the advent of motor trucks. *Courtesy the Bekins Company.*

much to operate per day, but could haul amost three times the ton-miles of a horse-drawn wagon of equal size.[15] The statistics of the truck's performance were even more impressive under adverse weather conditions. During a two-week heat wave in New York City that started on July 3, 1911, 1700 horses died from heat exhaustion, and thousands were disabled and rendered useless for future freighting duties.[16] Although these figures were higher than normal, similar incidents took place each summer: the average death rate in July for horses in New York City for the same period was almost 500 per week. Moreover, horses required one day of rest for each day of work. The motor truck was able to overcome these conditions and proved to be far superior in hauling perishable goods. Businessmen were forced to use ice to keep the milk, meat, and vegetables carried by horse-drawn wagons cool and fresh. A horseless carriage, hauling the same load, moved so quickly (by comparison) that products could be covered with wet burlap—

saving time, money, space, and weight.[17] During the winter in northern cities, ice and snow limited horses' dependability; the animals expended much of their energy trying to stay on their feet, and, with a heavy load, many horses lost their footing, resulting in broken or crippled legs. The introduction of traction chains for truck tires enabled motorized transportation to perform without a marked reduction in efficiency.[18]

Economy and concern for the noble horse swayed many Americans to accept the commercial automobile. However, the horse was not allowed to retain its honor as it retreated before a wave of technology. Truck lobbyists, not content with the long-range change to motorized freighting, tried to destroy the image of the horse. The horse, lambasted as a "purveyor of filth," [19] was charged with contributing to improper sanitation in the cities. Frequently traveled streets were pictured as "literally carpeted with a warm, brown matting of commuted horse-dropping, smelling to heaven and destined in no inconsiderable part to be scattered in fine dust in all directions, laden with countless millions of disease-bearing germs."[20] The lobbyists also argued that traffic congestion in cities would be relieved by using trucks. Fewer vehicles would be needed to carry the same amount of freight, and trucks occupied less space than horse-drawn wagons of the same carrying capacity. The space saved would be almost one-third in the street and almost two-thirds in the stable.[21]

With the approach of World War I, the horse found yet another adversary—proponents of increased war production.[22] President Woodrow Wilson believed he had to "train a nation for war," and, as the American people were encouraged to produce more and consume less, truck enthusiasts found a perfect example of waste: "Old Dobbin." Various estimates of the horse population in the United States in 1915 ranged from 25,000,000 to 30,000,000. Each consumed ten pounds of food for every hour it worked. Five acres of land, producing grain and hay, were required to feed the average horse each year; this same five acres of land could feed five people if converted to production of human food. More than 100 million people could be sustained on the land set aside for horse feed.[23]

In 1916, pro-automobile forces received aid from an unlikely

By 1910 the Auto Delivery Company in Portland, Oregon, could boast that it had the largest delivery system on the West Coast. *Courtesy the White Motor Corporation.*

source: the revolution that had started in 1910 in Mexico. This spilled over the boundary into the United States in March of 1916 when Pancho Villa conducted a bloody and unprovoked raid on Columbus, New Mexico. The American public and press clamored for a declaration of war in retaliation for the 17 Americans who were killed. Instead, President Woodrow Wilson sent an expeditionary force under the command of Brigadier General John J. "Black Jack" Pershing to pursue the Villistas and capture their leader. Although the Pershing Expedition was a military failure, it was a total transportation triumph for the young trucking industry.

Villa had an obvious advantage of fighting on a dry, desolate, familiar terrain. Pershing's major obstacle was providing transportation for his fighting force and maintaining a supply line 400 miles into the Mexican wilderness. To solve this problem "Black Jack" requested 100 trucks. Fewer than 1,000 trucks then were owned by the Army, and these were scattered across the United States;

Truck Company Number Eight transporting men and supplies in Mexico during the Pancho Villa campaign. *Courtesy the White Motor Corporation.*

moreover, truck manufacturers were hard pressed to fill war orders for the Allies fighting in Europe. In addition, the Army had not adopted a standard truck; manufacturers delivered the requested vehicles, but there were a total of 128 makes and models then among the Army's 1,000 trucks.

At the central repair shops and supply depots at Columbus, New Mexico, chaos reigned throughout the eleven-month campaign. Civilians were hired to drive and repair the trucks until the Army could recruit or train men.[24]

During the expedition, Pershing penetrated 400 miles into Mexico. Twenty-two transportation companies, each with twenty-five trucks, performed feats that out-dated the old war horse. The speed and reliability of these trucks, traveling through heat, dust, mud, and sand, proved the superiority of motorized transport. The Villa campaign demonstrated the need for more trucks in the Army. The lesson proved a valuable one, for on April 6, 1917, less

Open trucks provided scant protection for the civilians that were hired to drive supply trucks. *Courtesy the White Motor Corporation.*

than two months after Pershing was recalled from Mexico, Congress declared war against Germany and its Allies.[25]

The United States Army was ill-prepared to engage in a major conflict. There was a general shortage of men, supplies, and ammunitions. However, by the war's outbreak the Army owned 2,400 trucks and had some drivers, mechanics, and machines who had been tested against an elusive enemy in Mexico. This small number of trucks and men seemed insignificant in relation to the total war effort, but in relative terms, compared to the Army's arsenal of 1,500 machine guns and 55 airplanes, the Motor Transport Corps was well prepared. During World War I the truck and trucker provided excellent transportation for men and goods. The major problem was the insufficient number of vehicles shipped to Europe. Pershing pleaded with Washington to send more trucks and reported that for want of transportation his "situation was critical." Ambulances were not available to remove the wounded

Truck supply train supporting the American Army in Mexico in 1916. *Courtesy the White Motor Corporation.*

from battlefields. At another juncture he reported to the Chief of Staff that "our ability to supply and maneuver our forces depends largely on motor transportation . . . ,"[26] and that the shortage of trucks was embarrassing. The only way American forces were able to carry out their military plans was to borrow trucks and ambulances from the French army.

The newly created Motor Transport Corps had an abundance of other problems. Many of these, as in the Mexican campaign, were caused by the different makes and models of vehicles operated by the Army. At one point it was estimated that the Allies were using 213 different types of vehicles with 60,000 separate parts that could not be interchanged. Before the end of the war the Quartermaster Corps had evolved a solution: in "dough-boy" vernacular, the "Liberty truck." The Standard B heavy truck was developed by the Army independent of commercial models, and the light-duty White became the Army's Standard A.[27]

Such terrain slowed down the delivery of supplies and tested the ability of man and machine. *Courtesy the White Motor Corporation.*

The by-products of war were invaluable in increasing total truck sales in the United States. Photographs of the many applications of trucks in different phases of the war, the heroic efforts of the Transportation Corps, and appeals to the public to use trucks to haul much-needed food for the war effort advertised the motor truck to the world more than anything else ever would."[28] Before the United States entered the war, one writer had estimated the "white space value alone of the pictures printed in American newspapers and magazines . . . of the motor truck in the present European War would have cost the motor-truck industry of the United States a round sum of $15,000,000."[29]

Demands early in the war enabled truck manufacturers to sell their obsolete styles and equip their trucks with the same technological advances of passenger automobiles.[30] Many automobile plants maintained truck departments because a few trucks could be sold using the reputation of the passenger car. Wartime produced an array of specialty trucks: for moving big guns, tanks, and aircraft; as mobile homes for butcher shops, machine shops, and garages; as offices for telegraph, telephone, and radio; as electrotyping plants for making field maps; as field hospitals, and field kitchens; for water wagons, fire fighting, portable searchlights, troop transports, and ambulances. The usefulness and versatility of the truck in the war zone led to its wider use in peacetime.[31]

The war effort also resulted in greatly increased production and reduced consumption in America. The Fuel Administration pressed coal miners to produce more coal and the public to economize on heat. The public responded to propaganda in newspapers, on billboards, in pamphlets, and in speeches by increasing production. Nowhere was the increase and the effort to reach a surplus so great as with the Food Administration, headed by Herbert C. Hoover. Using a popular slogan, "Food Will Win The War—Don't Waste It," Hoover waged a propaganda campaign that demanded patriotism and self-sacrifice. Victory gardens were planted in backyards and empty lots to supply vegetables for the table, and different days of the week were proclaimed as wheatless, meatless, porkless, heatless, and lightless. Fuel production increased by two-fifths, and annual food shipments to Allied countries rose to three times the pre-war level.

As the nation reduced its consumption in order to ship goods to Europe, the primary transportation system in America proved inadequate. The railroads were not prepared for the massive increase in goods that needed to be moved from manufacturing centers to the nation's ports. All available equipment was pressed into service to move goods for export, and farm to market shipments suffered. By December of 1917 the transportation problem became so acute that President Wilson put the entire railroad system under governmental control. The Director General of Railroads operated the railroads as one giant system and speeded up the movement of goods. However, it was not the restructuring of the railroad operation alone that solved the problem; trucks began moving goods over routes that would not have been profitable before the war. Intercity, daily routes developed between principal cities along the eastern seaboard. The Army and Navy used truck convoys to deliver munitions and to transport personnel. Rural farm-to-town routes reduced railroad short-hauls and less-than-carload freight shipments. The flexibility and speed of the truck and the great demand for transport service during World War I proved that highway freight hauling could compete with the railroads.[32]

The federal government became interested in the nation's highways not only for the movement of goods but also for national defense. The Quartermaster Department requested the Council of National Defense to determine the best routes for Army truck movements in the United States. The National Highways Association, the American Automobile Association, and the American Association of State Highway Officials were actively lobbying in Congress for a national highway system paralleling the borders of the United States to speed the movement of troops, equipment, and munitions. After the war Herbert Hoover, when he became Secretary of Commerce in the Harding Administration, supported improved roads and increased truck transportation. He stated that, because of inadequate transportation from farm to market, "Fifty percent of our perishable foodstuffs never reach the consumer because the farms on which they are raised are too remote from the market at which they are sold. . . . By motor trucks the farmer will be able to reach better markets . . . , to spend more time actually producing on his farm and be able to sell food more cheaply by eliminating the present tremendous waste." [33]

The war also reduced the number of horses and mules because of their destruction in great numbers in the combat areas. However, the loss was not in the quantity but in the quality of the animals that were sent to the Allies in Europe. The best breeding stock from the United States was sent to be used in the war zone. From January 1, 1915, to the end of the war, 500,000 horses were sent to Europe, representing one-half the breeding stock in America. This wholesale destruction of horses led to a doubling in the price of horseflesh, and the cost of horse-drawn transportation was increased further by a rise in grain prices. Nor was the image of the horse enhanced in the war. The rigors of battlefield conditions demonstrated the reliability of the truck, and war correspondents and truck manufacturers lauded motorized warfare. Whereas the horse was rendered useless when struck by a bullet, the truck could withstand many direct hits and still operate. If the motorized vehicle was damaged, it could be repaired. The horse died. The day-to-day demand put on transportation under varied weather conditions proved the superiority of the truck.[34]

Trucks and their drivers became heroes during the war. They brought food and ammunition to the troops, and they carried the wounded to field hospitals. The majority of the trucks used by the Allied armies either were employed exclusively as ambulances or else carried wounded to field hospitals on their return trips from delivering supplies to the front. Perhaps the chambers of commerce across the nation should have followed the advice of truck enthusiasts: "Instead of immortalizing the heroes of the great war mounted on equine bronze, it will be more fitting to perpetuate their glorious deeds seated in armored automobiles."[35]

At the end of the "great war to end all wars," the anti-horse campaign was no longer needed. The truck had proven itself by patriotic service. When the troops came home, they brought truck-driving skills with them. Also, at the end of the war thousands of surplus trucks were released for private use. The performance of trucks in the war gave the boost needed to complete a second transportation revolution in America. In 1904, 700 trucks had been built in the United States; production had risen at a steady rate until 1914, when the total number reached 24,900 vehicles. However, at war's end the yearly truck production was more than 300,000.[36]

The motor truck had proven its usefulness in urban transportation and as an intercity mover of goods during the war. However, for the general public to accept the horseless carriage, better roads were needed. Prior to 1916 the overall condition of rural roads had not improved greatly since colonial times. Few states had highway departments, and the federal government did not have a general fund for financial support to road construction until 1916.

After the Civil War railroads had received public attention and governmental aid. As rails crisscrossed the continent, the farmer was able to ship his goods to market at a cheaper rate. However, the poor condition of roads required the farmer to live within 20 miles of market outlets in order to make productive use of his farm.[37] The primitive roads were impassable during much of the year.

Army maneuvers before World War I in Massachusetts. *Courtesy the White Motor Corporation.*

Spring rains reduced roadbeds to mud, and in winter the same roads became sheets of snow and ice. Because these conditions severely limited the farmer's market, many agriculturalists argued for better roads. However, the marked improvement in America's roads which came at the end of the 19th century was not in response to the farmers' plight but to the popularity of cycling. During the 1880s bicycles had been used by urban dwellers to escape cities for the more pleasant countryside; cycling became a sport for the rich and then for the growing middle class. Thus began the "good roads movement." Bicycle clubs combined to form a powerful lobby for highway development, but their activities were short lived. A new mania, automobile touring, then swept the nation, and the rich switched their allegiance to the more gentlemanly sport.

In the late 1890s and early 1900s, organized tours hurried into the country, scattering dust, gravel, and horses in their wake. These automobile drivers found the same conditions that had plagued farmers; in good weather the roads were passable, if the ruts could be avoided, mudholes had dried, and vehicles did not break down from the beating of the rough surface. Touring was reserved for the stout hearted and adventurous. As one writer noted, automobiles were "chiefly celebrated not for running but for their standing ability."[38] On each jaunt, extra tires, parts, and tools had to be carried. Chains and ropes were a must, tires had to be wrapped in ropes to gain extra traction through mud, and money was needed to hire a farmer's team if the ropes failed.[39]

The federal government took its first road census in 1904 to determine the condition and the improvements made on rural roads in America. Two million miles of roads existed, but only 141 miles were paved with tar, asphalt, or brick, and the roadbed had been improved on only 153,664 miles. The remaining roads were unimproved and bad. Improvements had been restricted to natural resources, size of state appropriations, and the ingenuity of the local road maintenance crews. Southerners had found burnt clay roads to be the cheapest and best for farmers. This system of spreading oil on the natural clay surface and then setting it on fire to reduce the stickiness dated back at least a thousand years. In coastal areas, planks or logs were laid across the roadbed to produce corduroy roads. However, gravel was the most common material used for road improvement; where there was little natural road material available, sawdust and straw were used. Sawdust was frequently spread over sandy soil eight to ten inches deep, and then a thin layer of sand was scattered over the top of the sawdust to prevent fires. Straw roads had a shorter life expectancy than sawdust, for fire was not the only problem; high winds scattered the straw, and, on at least one occasion, a herd of cows had eaten the improvements.[40]

The "Good Roads Movement" made little headway until automobile clubs, railroad companies, highway associations, and rural population came to its aid. Automobile clubs sought to convince the public and the federal government that hard-surfaced roads were essential to internal transportation in America. Their goal, to extend urban pavement to the countryside, would allow city dwellers to escape to the woodlands on weekends, providing wholesome recreation that could not be found in the cities. In addition, the farmer could bring his goods to market over the same road and enjoy the social and cultural amenities offered by urban centers. Lower food prices also would result. Farmers at first balked at such an idea. They seemed to feel that automobiles were playthings for the rich and had little practical use on the farm. However, as the good roads movement succeeded in getting demonstration roads built, farmers found that they could double their loads and reduce transportation time and expenses.

Railroad companies not only approved of the good roads movement, but also sponsored seedling miles—short stretches of paved surfaces—and transported road-building machinery free of charge. In areas where wagon roads were improved, all phases of transportation increased. The railroad was able to attract customers from as far as 60 miles away, and freight volume rose. Furthermore, during harvest time railroad cars had to be stockpiled at railheads in order to accommodate the great influx of farm commodities. When unimproved roads were reduced to mud or covered with ice, the farmer could not transport his goods, and the cars remained idle for weeks at a time.[41]

Highway construction companies had an obvious interest in the improvement of roads. They constructed many seedling miles at cost or free of charge to illustrate the advantages of hard-surfaced roads. As communities enjoyed the economic uplift

Before the 1930s transcontinental freighters traveled over unimproved wagon trails. *Courtesy the White Motor Corporation.*

brought by improved highways, "Good Road Days" were proclaimed, businesses closed for the day, farmers supplied draft animals to do the heavy work, and highway builders furnished construction equipment.[42]

During the first decade of the 20th century, road improvement was slow. Gradually, however, the farmers' attitude toward the automobile changed. Farmers at first had disliked the horseless carriage and the expenses associated with improving roads. Then automobiles became cheaper and more dependable, the rich traded in their old car for a newer model, and a used car market developed. The price of the automobile soon came within the economic grasp of the middle class.

The farmer did not buy a motorized wagon for touring, but

for more practical reasons. Used convertibles were the most popular vehicles. The touring body could be removed easily and replaced with a wooden truck body.[43] The popularity of such an adaptation resulted in several companies offering "form-a-truck" kits. These used touring cars-trucks offered several advantages over early trucks.[44] There were few used trucks for sale, and those were expensive; businesses did not trade in their trucks, but repaired them. When a technological improvement appeared on new models, it was adapted to older trucks. Furthermore, the enclosed cab of touring cars offered protection for the farmer's family on outings to the local village or town. Most often, the light trucks that the farmer would be interested in purchasing were assembled with an automobile frame and drive train; he thus saw little advantage to be gained by buying a truck. However, by the second decade of the 20th century there was a substantial reduction in truck prices, and light commercial vehicles, the forerunner of pickups, were purchased by farmers.[45]

The impact of the automobile on the farmer, measured in economic terms, was great. Transportation cost not only dictated the profit margin on most farms, but also was the single most important factor in assessing the value of farmland. In Sullivan County, Tennessee, for example, a farmer hauled one ton of wire 23 miles in 12 days at a cost of $36. Using a truck, the time was reduced to two hours and the cost to approximately $8.[46] The increase in agricultural shipments was equally impressive in those areas that had improved local roads. One study, conducted between 1909 and 1911 by the United States Office of Public Roads in Spottsylvania County, Virginia, showed that the rate of agricultural and forest tonnage arriving at the railhead in Fredericksburg increased 45 percent in the two years following the completion of 40 miles of surfaced roads. Moreover, a random sample of the price of farmland in the country for the same two-year period showed increases from more than 30 percent to more than 300 percent.[47]

The city dweller also benefited from improved farm-to-market roads. The farmer was able to ship perishable goods longer distances without the hazard of spoilage. Truck farms located near cities brought high rents for depleted land. Tenants paid $20 to

$30 per acre per year as rent for land adjacent to urban areas, while farmers located ten miles from the city rented more fertile land for three to four dollars per acre per year. In many cases, land further than ten miles from a city sold for the same amount as that paid in rent by an urban farmer in one year.[48] By 1920 it was common for a farmer to deliver goods to city markets 60 miles distant when 15 years earlier 10 miles would have been the maximum. The result was a rise in the standard of living for workers in the cities, and, at the same time, farmers were realizing profits from crops that previously could not be marketed. The price of fresh produce and dairy products plummeted.

Automobile mania thus infected many people in rural areas. Highway engineers, governmental agents, and popular magazines helped salesmen spread the evangelical word, "Buy an automobile and enjoy the luxuries and advantages of modern civilization." This intense propaganda for better roads and motorized highway transport did have some factual merit, but it was not a cure-all for the American farmer. However, high speed motorized transportation allowed the farmer to enjoy the trappings of the city and reduced the loneliness that previously had been associated with his rural life.[49] Before good roads, visiting a neighbor or the general store often consumed most of a day; the automobile reduced this time to less than an hour. Many women hated the day-to-day loneliness of farm life; as one contemporary social commentator put it, noting the abandonment of some farms, "The lack of social intercourse has proved a stronger factor in many cases than the sterility of the ground."[50] The one-room upgraded school began disappearing, replaced by a consolidated school which provided a better education. However, no greater effect on the social life of farmers was felt than the establishment of rural delivery by the Postmaster General in 1896. Postal routes were extended steadily as roads improved; the farmer was brought "within the daily range of the intellectual and commercial activities of the world, and the isolation and monotony which have been the bane of agricultural life sensibly mitigated."[51]

Every aspect of the farmer's social life was studied by those interested in the positive impact of good roads and motorized transportation. Vast improvements in mental and physical health were pictured for those who could not be swayed with intellectual and economic gains. Riding in an automobile after a day's work allowed "the unstringing of high tensioned nerves. . . ." What the nervous farmer needed was a "flight over smooth and undulating roads" to bring "rest with relaxation, and cure with comfort."[52] To gain the full benefits of the automobile, its owner should escape "to the roads, to the hills, to the country with their varied shades of living carpets, with freshening winds and glad'ning brooks, with bees, and birds, and flowers into nature's great laboratory where are brewed nectars and panaceas for the ills which infest mankind."[53] The rural population believed what they read, and the popularity of the horseless carriage among farmers seemed boundless. Henry Ford reported that he had to chain his car to a lamp post to stop inquisitive passersby from taking it for a spin. One writer in a popular journal predicted that the automobile would bring "health, wealth, optimism, and a brighter future"[54] to the American farmer. A farmer's wife, when asked why her family would spend a large sum of money for an automobile when they did not have indoor plumbing, retorted, "You can't go to town in a bathtub."[55]

As roads extended to rural areas, trucks were able to utilize these new routes of commerce. However, intercity freight hauling was not economically feasible until state governments, with the aid of large federal appropriations, extended the few miles of farm-to-market roads across county lines and connected major cities. Few independent truckers wanted to haul freight over unimproved roads, although tire manufacturers, truck promoters, and proponents of the good roads movement did sponsor numerous transcontinental trips. Man and machine fought mud, inadequate bridges, high water, and mechanical failure to prove that trucks were practical modes of transportation. In 1911 a Swiss-built Sauger became the first truck to make a transcontinental journey across the United States. The driver left Denver on the first leg and traveled for 66 days to reach Los Angeles; the truck then was shipped by rail to Pueblo, Colorado, to start its journey to New York. Newspaper and magazine coverage of the trip proved valuable and was cheap advertising. However, the record was short-lived, for the following year a Packard truck sped from New York to San Francisco with a three-ton load in 46 days.[56]

In 1916 one of the more unusual transcontinental trips was undertaken. William Warwick, his wife, and younger daughter left Seattle, Washington, in a one and one-half ton GMC truck, intending to deliver a ton of Carnation Milk to New York. The trip was sponsored by the Seattle Chamber of Commerce to advertise the National Parks Transcontinental Highway. The Warwicks hoped to make the trip to prove that this highway could accommodate automobile tourists. Morever, the free advertising gained from such an unusual trip would attract sufficient tourist trade to Seattle to offset the cost of sponsoring the trip.[57] During the journey the driver could not accept any help when stuck, nor was he allowed to use chains, ropes, or planks. The truck did not have any special equipment, carrying only a standard tool kit.

On July 12 the truck headed east. For ten weeks Warwick struggled across the continent, digging the truck out of mud holes, rebuilding broken bridges, and appealing to local citizens for road improvement. During the 3,710-mile trip, he broke 43 bridges and culverts. In all the trip proved a failure. Transcontinental tourist and freight traffic had to wait for federal funding for roads before Seattle's dream could become a reality.[58]

Out of the Mud and
Onto the Concrete

The inability of railroads to carry a sudden increase in traffic during World War I magnified the need for better highways in the United States. Although cyclists, automobile enthusiasts, and farmers had made some headway prior to 1916, the major obstacle was archaic local and state laws concerning road improvements. Until 1891 the maintenance and construction of highways in the states were the responsibility of landowners in townships, counties, or engineering districts adjacent to a road. Each citizen in the district was taxed a fixed amount each year for road maintenance; he had the option of paying the sum in cash or personally working out his payment on the road. Most often a road day was proclaimed, and members of a community would gather outside of town with shovels, rakes, and picnic baskets to "play in the mud." [1] New Jersey, typical of most other states, had few roads that were improved. Truck farmers relied on the market in nearby large cities, especially New York and Philadelphia; freighting to those distant markets over poorly constructed and maintained roads represented a great loss both in time and money. By 1891, farmers, with support from the State Board of Agriculture and the governor, had secured passage of the State Aid Law. The State of New Jersey thereby assumed one-third of the cost of construction, the property owner paid one-tenth, and the county was responsible for the remaining sum.[2]

The precedent established in New Jersey was followed by Massachusetts in 1893. Its first law for the building and maintenance of state highways between cities provided that counties would grade the roads and the state would pave them. The following year the state highway commission took charge of improvements and charged the county 25 percent of the cost of construction. The success of such aid in highway construction resulted in a majority of the states passing similar laws.[3]

Most states originally authorized money for road construction to come from the general revenue fund, but as the advantages of improved roads were realized the public demanded increased action. Highway building mushroomed. By January 1, 1914, the total indebtedness of states and counties for highway and bridge bonds was $445,147,073. Moreover, wartime traffic put a heavier stress on existing roads, and the states responded with yet more funds. During a 13-month period commencing on November 1, 1918, the total of all approved and pending state highway bonds amounted to more than $500,000,000.[4]

The federal government was slow to become involved, for few states wanted to relinquish to the central government their power to build roads. This previously had been an important issue. At the end of the 19th century, the nation's roads had been the subject of discussion among many Congressmen, and in 1893, a bill had been introduced in the House of Representatives "instructing the committee on agriculture to incorporate in the agricultural appropriation the sum of $15,000 to be expended for the purpose of making investigations for a better system of roads."[5] In response, the committee on agriculture had drafted a statute creating the Office of Public Roads with a budget of $10,000.[6]

J. Sterling Morton, the Secretary of Agriculture, had appointed a prominent civil engineer, General Roy Stone, as director of the Office of Public Roads. On October 3, 1893, General Stone had received instructions for supervising this investigation of American roads. He was to study road management systems in the various states, find the best methods of road construction, publish and distribute his findings, and aid agricultural colleges and experiment stations in spreading news of scientific construction techniques. Stone was warned that the states or localities should shoulder the expense of building all roads; he was not to exercise undue influence or control over the building of any highway system, nor was he to attempt to furnish labor for the construction of any road. Any infraction of such orders would result in "hostile criticism" by the Secretary of Agriculture.[7]

Stone's office sent agents to give speeches, conduct "good roads" seminars, and supervise the building of object roads. Moreover, he encouraged the organization and activities of good roads associations by printing future convention dates and proceedings of the meetings. Professional and scientific organizations that studied road construction also received attention from his office. Data collected by the American Society for Testing Materials, the American Society of Civil Engineers, the Bureau of Standards, and other professional organizations was published in the *Bulletin*.[8] When the Department of Agriculture reorganized in 1915, the Office of Public Roads was given the responsibility of all engineering within the Department. With this new objective, the office added the words "and Rural Engineering" to its title. The following year the Federal Road Act was passed, and again new goals were set. The office was responsible for educating the public by lectures; it also was to publish the findings of scientific research, to build model roads, to engage in research, to improve existing methods of construction and testing of construction materials, and to administer the Federal Road Act of 1916.[9]

Since 1904 Congress annually had attempted to pass federal appropriations for road construction. The arguments advanced against federal aid by Congressmen opposed to such a bill included infringement on states rights, as well as statements that any large appropriation not only would result in isolated cases of pork barrelism, but also would fail to improve the general condition of roads. However, petitions, letters, and lobbyists representing the good roads movement spurred Congressmen to introduce 49 bills during the 63rd Congress alone. To resolve the problem, a joint Congressional committee was appointed to study the many possible solutions. The final report was submitted on January 21, 1915. Statistics gathered about the condition of rural highways, highway expenditures, comparative cost of road construction, state debts incurred from highway construction, and the possible effect federal aid would have on existing transportation were impressively in favor of federal aid.[10]

The chairman of the committee on roads presented a proposed bill for federal aid on January 6, 1916. This bill, after debate and approval by both houses of Congress, was signed by President Woodrow Wilson on July 11, 1916. The amended title was "An Act to provide that the United States shall aid the States in the construction of rural post roads, and for other purposes." For the sake of brevity it was most often called simply "The Federal-Aid Road Act." The bill authorized the Secretary of Agriculture to work with state highway departments to determine which rural post roads should be improved and what type of materials would be used in their construction. However, before any state could receive funds, it would have to agree to the constitutionality of the law. To give a wider application to the bill, rural post roads were redefined to include all routes over which the United States mail was carried and any future routes that might be used for delivery. A rural area was defined as a place with a population of less than 2,500 inhabitants, unless houses were separated by more than two hundred feet. Moreover, any highway that was constructed under the act would have to be free of tolls.[11]

The total appropriation, providing matching funds to be spread out over five fiscal years, was $75 million. In the first year, ending June 30, 1917, $5 million could be spent, and each year thereafter another $5 million would be added to the amount until in 1921 the total would be $25 million. Allocations to a state were based on its percentage of land area, its population, and its miles of rural delivery routes in relation to the national average. An additional $10 million was allocated for construction and maintenance of roads in national forests, the roads to be used primarily by companies extracting national resources from public lands.[12]

From this meager beginning, federal aid to state highway construction gradually grew to mammoth proportions. All segments of society were eager to bring about the affluent, mobile society; to facilitate this movement, concrete and asphalt carpets soon stretched across the nation.

An amendment to the original Federal Road Act was added in 1919. The Post Office Appropriation Act that year provided for an additional expenditure of $200 million for construction and maintenance of post roads. The first year $50 million would be allocated, and $75 million would be spent in the two following fiscal years. Moreover, funds for forest roads were approved: $9 million to be equally divided among the three fiscal years. To speed construction of new highways and to protect the trucking industry's expanding market, the act also provided that surplus war material and equipment that could be used for road construction would be transferred to the Department of Agriculture. By the fall of 1921 that department had received 24,353 vehicles and a large quantity of spare parts. The various state highway departments eagerly accepted this equipment and adapted it to road construction: ambulances became portable offices and light delivery wagons; trucks were altered to become snowplows and scrapers; and other vehicles were fitted with watering tanks, dump beds, and benches. The golden era of road construction then began.[13]

During the 1920s federal funding spurred highway construction. Annual investments in roads changed from millions to billions. As each section of federal-aid highway was completed, the demand for feeder roads from farmers, businessmen, and truckers increased. Although the need for improved highways was apparent, most states and counties did not have a general transportation policy. A county of state highway would be improved to a political boundary without regard to the condition of the road across the line; this inhibited intercounty and interstate traffic. Highways were constructed parallel to railroads or water routes, but at the same time remote areas were neglected. Moreover, the number of interstate highway routes was acutely insufficient. This had become apparent during World War I, when the military struggled to transport men and supplies across the nation, and Congress felt compelled to prepare for the next national emergency by incorporating strategic military transport routes into the federal highway systems. Congress recognized these inconsistencies and believed inadequate planning was inherent where state and local governments controlled transportation policies. In an effort to eliminate such planning, the Federal Highway Act of 1921 limited the number of roads that could be improved to seven percent of the total rural mileage in a state and approved aid only to those roads that were designed for interstate or intercounty traffic.[14]

The highway appropriation of $75 million for fiscal year 1922 was approximately the annual average for the next eight years. State and local governments during the same period spent in excess of $17 billion for construction and maintenance to raise the total highway expenditures to more than $20 billion for the decade ending in 1931. The "Great Depression" provided an opportunity for a great increase in federal and state funding. The sad state of the nation's economy during the depression resulted in emergency governmental funding for public works. Increased highway construction provided an outlet for governmental spending and thousands of jobs for the unemployed. Up to 1930 the total federal aid allocated to highway construction amounted to $790 million. However, President Franklin D. Roosevelt's social betterment policies poured out more than $2.2 billion of federal money for highway improvement. Interstate highways received only a small percentage of the funding, while most states boasted of vastly improved farm-to-market roadbeds.[15]

From 1940 to 1943 road construction was at a standstill. The war consumed the energies of the nation, and the increased war traffic and neglect of highway maintenance brought about passage of the Federal Aid Highway Act in 1944. This measure contained many of the same elements as the Bill of 1921, but added funds for urban centers with a population of more than 5,000 and established an interstate system that was not to be more than 41,000 miles in length. A total of $1.5 billion was allocated to be doled out to the states over a three-year period. The urban system was to receive 25 percent of the allocation, the secondary system 30 percent, and the primary rural highways, which included the Interstate System, the remaining 45 percent. For the first time a comprehensive, federal highway system was planned.[16]

The annual federal expenditures remained fairly constant until the passage of the Federal Aid Act of 1956. Congress believed that the $500 million average expenditure was not enough for rapid completion of the interstate system, and additional funds were made available. A total of $24,625 billion was allocated for fiscal years 1957-1969. Funds were distributed under the same percentage guidelines as in the Act of 1944, but the cost of constructing the Interstate System to the states was reduced. Instead of providing matching funds, the states would pay only 10 percent of the total cost incurred in construction of interstate routes. This vast Interstate System was to be completed by 1972, but in 1968 an additional 1,500 miles were added to the 41,000 miles that had been planned initially, and the completion date was moved forward to 1977. Moreover, the cost had risen from $24 billion to more than $100 billion—and the estimates for final completion continue to rise. The limited-access, super highways were planned to provide a transportation system that would accommodate the estimated traffic flow that would develop by 1975. Again the government underestimated the growth of private automobile travel and of commercial motor freighting.[17]

Funding for this expensive network of roads came by creating the Highway Trust Fund. Taxes on lubricating oils, tires, and gasoline, combined with excise taxes paid by buses and trucks, provided a users' tax to build new highways. Thus the fund was self-perpetuating; as new highways were built, more automobile miles were logged, and more funds were collected to build more highways.

The demand for new and improved highways, along with bigger and more comfortable automobiles and trucks, appeared insatiable. In 1971 alone more than $20 billion was spent on highways, more than $27 billion on new vehicles, and more than a trillion miles were traveled. The farmer, tourist, and trucker had been pulled out of the mud, the city dweller had been relocated in suburbia, and the trust fund was generating more income. By 1973 the Federal Highway Trust Fund, established in 1956, had spent $63 billion, of which more than $40 billion had gone for construction of the Interstate System. The Interstate System had received the bulk of federal expenditures, while the primary, secondary, and urban systems had expanded to include 870,000 miles. Moreover, in 1975 the matching-fund status employed on the other-than-Interstate-construction was changed; the state's burden was reduced to 30 percent, and, starting with fiscal year 1976, the primary system would include those routes that extended the Interstate into urban areas and the major traffic routes that fed large volumes of traffic to existing Interstate routes.[18]

Rubber on Concrete

The emergence of long-haul trucking awaited the construction of roadways, the development of machines and tires, and the economic necessity for extending urban motor freighting to the countryside. The early long-haul was used primarily to expose how dreadful were the roads, how dependable were the trucks, and the durability of tires. The first successful transcontinental run was made in 1911 by a Sauger truck, but the two-month test showed the poor conditions of roads, bridges, and culverts and the enduring strength of drivers. Subsequent overland treks were undertaken for the same purpose, and world records were claimed by each truck manufacturer as the total time for the trip was reduced from months and weeks to days and hours. Truckers should have received world records for repairing and over-hauling and pushing and pulling their unwilling mechanical beasts across a continent.[1]

During the expedition in 1916 against Pancho Villa, the major problem was inadequate tires. At the turn of the century heavy trucks used steel or wooden tires, but with improvements in tire casting and rim design they soon rode on solid rubber tires. As long as trucks maintained speeds of less than ten miles per hour and were traveling on good roadways, solid tires were serviceable. In sand, mud, or loose gravel, solid tires, because of their narrow width, would either sink, become stuck, or lose traction. At speeds approaching 15 miles per hour, a truck with solid tires would vibrate, not only shaking the cargo to such an extent that much of it

Older style bridges often gave way under heavy loads. *Courtesy the White Motor Corporation.*

was damaged beyond salvage, but also limiting the ability of the driver to control the vehicle. The ill effects of the solid tire limited the speed of service for long-distance cargo hauling and greatly increased the rate of kidney and back disorders, not to mention the many cases of chipped teeth among operators of those "bone rattlers." Governmental agencies that maintained roads frequently used by trucks added to the complaints levied at solid tires. Their lack of absorbing qualities destroyed road surfaces, and in many regions trucks were restricted from using surfaced highways.

Pneumatic tires offered an alternative. In the 1890s bicycle makers had utilized air-filled tires with a rubber and cotton exterior and double innertubes to provide a cushioned ride. These tires were adapted to the automobile with little change in construction or size. However the extra weight and increased speed of an

Typical Army truck used during the Pancho Villa expedition in 1916. *Courtesy the White Motor Corporation.*

automobile reduced tire life; improvements in tread design and wider tires had to be introduced before the pneumatic could become standard equipment on automobiles. The softer ride and increased handling ability these brought appealed to the American consumer, and by 1916 half of all automobile tires sold were pneumatics. The same convenience was not offered to truck owners. The cloth, reinforced pneumatics could not withstand heavy loads and the resulting punishment that came from roads riddled with chuckholes. The same year that automobile pneumatics outsold solid tires, truck owners bought one pneumatic for every 60 solids.[2]

Goodyear Tire and Rubber Company of Akron, Ohio, developed a new design for pneumatics that used a strong rubber cord substitute for cloth reinforcement. This could withstand the

Hard rubber tires and heavy loads made these early "bone rattlers" difficult to drive. *Courtesy the Kenworth Motor Truck Company.*

demands placed on tires by heavy trucks. In order to test the tire under actual long-haul conditions, P. W. Litchfield, Goodyear's plant manager, started a regular trucking route from Akron to Boston. The first truck, dubbed the Wingfoot Express in honor of the Goodyear Trademark, left Akron on its first non-stop trip on April 9, 1917. The scheduled time for the run was seven days. This proved an optimistic forecast. The Goodyear Company's press releases reported that the trucking route was established not only to show the higher speeds, greater economy, increased traction, and smoother ride offered by the new corded pneumatic tires, but also to engage in carrying tires from Akron to the Eastern market and

As late as 1923 hard rubber tires were still being used on heavy duty trucks. *Courtesy the White Motor Corporation.*

returning to Akron with cotton fabric from Goodyear's mills at Killingly, Connecticut.[3]

As with the sailors, soldiers of fortune, and explorers of earlier days, two single men were chosen for this adventure, which would take them over the 700 miles from the urban pavements of Akron to the distant East. Harry Smeltzer had gained some experience driving a truck equipped with cord pneumatics but only on short hauls. His traveling companion, Harry Apple, had no such advantage. The new Packard truck used for that first trip had no special equipment except cord pneumatics inflated to 110 pounds pressure and a sleeping compartment that ran the width of the cab. On the first trip the only cargo was extra tires, oil, gasoline, and an air compressor. Two Packard cars accompanied Smeltzer and Apple on the trip to help in case of breakdown and to provide transportation for the Goodyear public relations team. Goodyear provided a tire engineer, garage manager, and race car driver, and Packard sent along two factory engineers to repair the truck.[4]

Early on the morning of April 9, 1917, this historic caravan embarked on the first major interstate trucking enterprise. The three vehicles sped through the Ohio countryside for three hours logging an uneventful 25 miles—until the pavement ran out at Edinburg. After negotiating the muddy road for one mile, the truck gave up the struggle. For the rest of the day the crew constructed a platform from material gathered from a nearby farmer's rail fence, but still failed to get the truck out of the mud. Relying on a custom established in early touring days, the stranded motorists spent the night at a farmer's house. The following morning, with the help of a borrowed winch, the truck was extracted and continued on its way.[5]

Mud was not the most difficult hurdle to overcome on the journey. The rough roads and long hours strained both men and machine. On an average, for every 50 miles of travel one of the pneumatics would blow out. At Jeanette, Pennsylvania, the truck engine failed, and the trip eastward had to be postponed for five days to wait for a new engine to arrive and then to be installed. Even with the new motor and the assistance of factory mechanics, the engine failed and was overhauled in Philadelphia and again in Boston, causing further delays. The Packard truck, with its travel-weary crew, triumphantly entered Killingly, Connecticut, 16 days behind schedule.[6]

Goodyear had provided advance publicity and a band was engaged to give a grand welcome to the pioneer voyagers. Smeltzer and Apple, veterans of the open road, surprisingly made a relatively easy five-day return trip to Akron by truck. Subsequent trips were made with cargoes of rubber products for the East, with return loads of cotton fabric. By the third trip the seven-day schedule was met, and by summer a five-day round trip was standard. Although the first trip consumed 28 days and 28 tires, later trips proved that not only were pneumatics superior to solid tires but also that long-haul trucking was economically feasible. Further-

Goodyear's Akron-Boston Express. *Courtesy the Goodyear Tire and Rubber Company.*

more, the press releases of the Akron-Boston Express route and the advertisement scrolled in bold letters on Goodyear trucks helped popularize new tires and interstate trucking.[7]

Goodyear continued to promote its tires with the aid of long-distance runs. In 1918 truck convoys carried 18 tons of tires to Chicago, Boy Scouts on a 3,000 mile tour of the South, and Red Cross supplies from Chicago to Baltimore. Each trip provided excellent free advertisement for a new cord pneumatic tire and increased interest in interstate trucking. During the fall that same year of 1918, Goodyear capped its advertising campaign with a delivery of aircraft tires to San Francisco. The struggle across the nation tested the mettle of men and machine, but did not show promise for future transcontinental trucking. The trucks logged 7,763 miles, destroyed 36 bridges, and traveled more miles over unimproved trails than surfaced roads.[8]

As Goodyear tested tires in America, the United States Army

A convoy of Goodyear trucks enroute between Akron and Boston.
Courtesy the Goodyear Tire and Rubber Company.

tested trucks under wartime conditions in Europe. Many of the
trucks and men used in the campaign against Pancho Villa in
Mexico made their way to Europe and were engaged in general
transport duties under the command of "Black Jack" Pershing.
With the creation of the Motor Transport Corps, the Army wedded its transportation needs to the truck. General Pershing estimated that 50,000 trucks would be needed, but throughout the
conflict his request for additional vehicles was lost in the Department of War's red tape and stalled by the inability of the Merchant
Marines to deliver all the needed war supplies.[9]

Pershing was shocked that the United States, the largest pro-
ducer of motor vehicles in the world, could not fill his request for
more trucks and that when transportation bottlenecks developed
he had to borrow trucks from the French. Moreover, in the summer of 1918 Pershing was refused the use of the French vehicles
because the French were in the process of asking the same favor

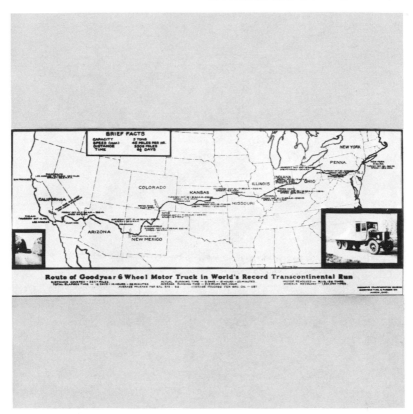

Route of Goodyear's world's record transcontinental run. *Courtesy the Goodyear Tire and Rubber Company.*

from Americans. Conditions became critical when a shortage of ambulances made the transfer of wounded from the front lines to field hospitals almost impossible. The problem was compounded when 20 new hospital units arrived without any means to transport the wounded.[10]

The difficulties of transportation in a war zone during World War I seemed insurmountable. The logistics of freighting men, munitions, and food to the front lines and maintaining 200 odd makes and models of trucks, which had more than 60,000 separate parts, taxed the Motor Corps. A large majority of the drivers and mechanics had little if any experience in transportation. Efforts to recruit drivers met with some success; the Motor Truck Club of

Goodyear drivers had to repair dozens of bridges on their struggle West. *Courtesy the Goodyear Tire and Rubber Company.*

America organized a recruiting drive which resulted in 1,400 chauffeurs being mustered into the Army. However, most drivers gained their experience behind the wheel of a truck on the front lines. Early in the year truckers developed many of the habits that would be the trademark of future long-haul drivers.[11]

Drivers faced long hours of monotonous driving over battle-scarred roads made practically impassable by the many vehicles that had gouged the earth into deep ruts. Open cabs provided scant protection from the elements, and the shortage of trucks left little time for exhausted drivers to rest. Hours stretched into days as long supply trains shuttled to and from supply depots and front lines. One such group of men, members of the Hundred and

Motor Truck Company No. 2 which transversed 300 miles of wilderness to keep American troops supplied with rations and ammunition during the Mexican campaign. *Courtesy the White Motor Corporation.*

Seventeenth Supply Train of Texas, symbolized the romantic and often colorful nature that became the trademark of Army truckers. In September of 1918, as Pershing lamented his critical shortage of trucks, the Hundred and Seventeenth inched its way toward the French front. Each of the 200 trucks was manned by a pair of Texas rebels, including a mixture of experience-hardened veterans and those that had "been used to the soft life."[12]

Convoy duty meant days and nights of travel without knowledge of when or where the trip might end. At night the truckers, running without lights, followed the tailgate of the truck in front, mesmerizing the drivers and adding to the dream-like quality of events brought about by mental and physical fatigue. The long line of trucks moving at a slow pace would halt, drivers would stretch numb muscles and consume what rations were available, and then, at the sound of a whistle, resume their trip to some unknown destination. Cognac-filled canteens gave some relief from the cold, driving rain that soaked the cargo, drenched the drivers, and made the roads a sea of mud. Constant vibration and bone-jarring lurches of the steering wheel sapped the men's strength but relieved the monotony of constant driving.[13] As drivers delivered much-needed supplies to the front lines and returned the wounded to hospitals, the American press captured the heroic and romantic nature of the newly created Motor Corps and predicted the coming of a transportation revolution.

The favorable image of this new form of transportation was easily contrasted with the monopolistic tendencies of railroads. Not only did the truck replace the Army horse on convoy duty, but also the truck replaced the iron horse on short hauls. The routes most often began in the major urban manufacturing centers and radiated out to smaller cities within 50 miles. A few exceptions to that rule were trucks that plied between the large industrial cities along the eastern seaboard. However, the most enduring change wrought by trucking during the war was the delivery of farm products to the cities to alleviate the food shortage caused by congested rails.[14]

The government helped increase truck traffic by not limiting the production of large pneumatic tires, and the Railroad Administration actively supported less-than-carload shipments by truck. Posters were placed in railroad freight offices suggesting that shippers use trucks for small shipments and for perishable items. Moreover, the Council of National Defense eliminated the costly empty back haul by establishing bureaus to coordinate cargo shipments and provide return loads for truckers. The major tire manufacturers supported the government's actions and benefited from the increased truck transportation through greater tire sales. Harvey S. Firestone came to the aid of highway and national transportation through his stroke of genius: a "Ship-by-Truck" advertising campaign. Good roads and regularly scheduled runs increased truck traffic, reduced rail congestion—and sold more tires.[15]

The Firestone Company spent more than $2 million promot-

The Army Motor Corps gaining valuable experience during the Mexican campaign. *Courtesy the White Motor Corporation.*

ing its ship-by-truck campaign. The system of bureaus set up by the Council of National Defense to coordinate traffic and help locate return loads for truckers was abandoned at war's end, but was reestablished by the Firestone Company. The 67 branches it set up to provide information, conduct research, and distribute literature about the trucking industry also provided return loads for back hauls. Each branch was to promote the construction of better roads and to lobby for uniform state laws for interstate traffic. Firestone sent a fleet of trucks through the South to promote trucking and to gain free advertising. Most of the publicity paid for by Firestone and appearing in local newspapers pointed out that trucks would reduce the cost of operating a business, thereby reducing the general cost of living for everyone. The railroads inadvertently aided trucking by going on general strike in 1920, just days before the beginning of a national "Ship-by-Truck Good Roads Week."[16]

The alliances established during World War I between tire

producers and the trucking industry continued to prosper into the 1930s and 1940s. Both industries were adversely affected by the postwar economic depression of 1921 and 1922, but, as politicians had promised, prosperity was just around the corner. Truck sales decreased from a record-setting 300,000 in 1920 to less than half that figure in 1921. However, the recovery was apparent when, for the first time, total sales reached 400,000 in 1923, and the tire industry ushered in the jazz age with the development of balloon tires.[17] The first cord pneumatics had reduced many of the problems encountered with solid rubber tires, but the high pressure required in those tires reduced tire wear, increased blowouts, and retained many of the other engineering problems of the solid tire. Moreover, the tires were narrow in width, requiring the diameter of tires to increase with the carrying capacity of the truck. As tires increased in size, the height of the axle increased accordingly, making it impossible to build a loading platform of standard size for maximum loading efficiency.[18]

The balloon tire used the same basic air support system as cord pneumatics, but the same volume of air was displaced within a larger tire casting. The load rested on a cushion of air instead of a rigid tire. This new design resulted in the tire becoming a container for air instead of a load support system. Thus the new tire eliminated the extremely high air pressure per square inch previously needed, and it greatly decreased the possibility of blowouts and the high incidence of tread wear. The advantages were clear: the increased surface of the tire gave greater traction, and the lower air pressure allowed the tires to absorb most of the vibrations caused by small bumps in the road. Higher speeds could be maintained because of the general reduction in vibrations and road shocks.[19] Moreover, new processes for bonding rubber, cotton cord, and steel reinforcement into one unit and advances in mass production brought a superior and more economical tire. The average mile-cost for tires thereby was reduced from one cent per mile in 1918 to one-tenth of that cost in 1930.[20] Advances in tire manufacturing, good roads, veteran drivers trained during the war, and, thanks to a good press, public acceptance brought changes to the industry—which also benefited from mechanical advances in truck building.

Daily truck freighting services developed between major cities with the start of World War I. *Courtesy the White Motor Corporation.*

Technological advances included more than tires, which spurred other improvements because trucks equipped with them could maintain higher speeds for longer distances. Mechanical engineers began searching for greater operational efficiency in order to gain a competitive edge in the market place. Major truck manufacturing firms invested millions of dollars in research and development to create more efficient engines and metallurgy. The new metals developed were stronger and lighter, which led to a corresponding reduction in wear and weight. Powder metallurgy allowed many parts to be cast in close to finished form, eliminating

The White assembly line in 1925. *Courtesy the White Motor Corporation.*

some costly machine tooling. Moreover, many of the major parts of large trucks became standardized so that they were interchangeable and could be used as long as ten years.[21]

Between the two world wars, trucks became more efficient transports, and, at the same time, the average cost per truck was greatly reduced. Manufacturing advances and the economy of scale had a strong impact on initial cost reductions. Before World War I the number of trucks produced annually was fewer than 100,000, but averaged more than 500,000 units per year between the wars. Production was not greatly affected by the Great Depression; in

Interchangeable parts reduced the costs of trucks and lowered repair bills. *Courtesy the White Motor Corporation.*

only two years did sales dip below 300,000 units. A record 891,000 trucks were sold in 1937.[22] Truck sales owed much to external conditions not affected by manufacturing improvements. The large network of improved roads enabled highway transportation to develop where railroads had enjoyed a monopoly and in regions where other types of transport either were not available or else were archaic. Nevertheless, trucking would not have developed without the greater durability and increased speed offered by the technologically improved truck.

During the two decades following World War I, the price of trucks was reduced by half. The price for an engine of equal horsepower rating was reduced by four-fifths, but could be expected to operate for three times as long as the earlier engine. Other major components found on a truck had similar reductions in cost. Increased gas mileage and horsepower came with the introduction of higher grade motor oils during the early 1930s. The

Chain drive and hard rubber tires on these 1918 Whites became obsolete equipment during the next decade. *Courtesy the White Motor Corporation.*

lighter weight oil reduced engine wear and, at the same time, maintained its viscosity at higher temperatures and provided a greater ease in starting during cold weather. Steel alloys produced additional strength and life expectancy in axles, universal joints, and gear teeth. Refinements in carburetors, reduced wheel diameters, and replacement of the chain drive with a solid driveshaft gave trucks greater power utilization. The end result was a higher quality product that could transport goods at a cheaper per-ton-mile cost.[23]

Although gasoline engine design was not radically altered, truck engine development in the 1930s foretold the future. The diesel truck engine was first introduced in 1931 by Cummins and promised to give better service at a cheaper operational cost. However, the initial cost was much higher than for a comparable gasoline engine, and repairing the engine required special tools and trained mechanics. Because the diesel motor had fewer work-

During the first two decades of trucking, trailers had changed little from their horse-drawn counterpart. *Courtesy the White Motor Corporation.*

ing parts and burned less fuel, it became popular with long-haul truckers.

In the 1920s also came increased load capacity for trucks. Multi-geared transmissions and two-speed axles enabled trucks to maintain engine speed at peak performance and transmit the power from the engine to the rear wheels without substantial loss of power. Speed could be maintained on hills and, at the same time, decrease strain on the engine. Moreover, advancements in trailer construction and design gave better load capacity and greater utilization of the improvements in engines and transmissions. At first, trailers were not distinguishable from farm wagons. By 1920, a majority of truck-drawn trailers had lost their front axles and were attached to the truck by a hitch.[24] The development of modern trailers allowed small trucks to pull large loads. Moreover, once the truck cab could be freed of its trailer, it became more flexible. A large, straight-body truck had far less maneuverability than a tractor and trailer combination, cost less than before, and provided a more economical operation.

As with other technological improvements in the trucking industry, the greatest advances in trailer construction came immediately following World War I. Before 1920, attaching and releasing a loaded trailer required several men, hydraulic jacks, and considerable time, but with the introduction of the automatic fifth wheel in 1920, the operation was accomplished with ease. A practical application of power-assisted air brakes for trailers appeared in 1924, enabling the driver to control jack-knifing and to stop in shorter distances. Pneumatic tires and higher quality springs reduced road shock, and the weight of the trailers continued to decline with the replacement of heavy iron supports with lighter steel alloys. The use of the heavy solid axles ended when I-beam construction, giving added strength with lighter weight to trailers, made it possible to use tubular axles. The 1930s brought more advancements, many of them borrowed from the aircraft industry. Aluminum and stainless steel replaced heavier metals, and trailer manufacturers used the principle employed in airplane fuselage building to produce frameless trailers. Before the end of the decade, the trailer industry followed the truck manufacturers' practice of standardization, thus greatly reducing manufacturing cost.[25]

Improvements in truck design, durability, and manufacturing techniques were conceived with economy of operation in mind, not the creature comfort of the driver. However, many of these improvements reduced the workload of the driver and provided greater ease of handling. Prior to 1920 truck driving not only required a great amount of mechanical knowledge, but also an abundance of physical strength and endurance. The typical truck cab resembled a dray wagon's riding platform. Without the protection afforded by a cab, teamsters were at the mercy of the changing elements. Rain, snow, mud, and bugs found a resting place on the weary driver as he sat on the wooden bench and operated the tiller. During the first 20 years of trucking, few vehicles offered any

By 1913 trailers had taken on a modern-day appearance. *Courtesy the White Motor Corporation.*

protection for the driver—and then conditions became progressively worse. When higher speeds and an extended radius of operation became possible, the trucker faced longer hours, increased wind velocity, and more bad roads.[26]

On each trip the driver was fearful of a mechanical breakdown with little expectation of help. When extra parts, a well-equipped tool box, and an extensive—and colorful—vocabulary did not fix the ailing mechanical beast, the driver had to be prepared to spend the night where he was and resume work the next morning. Hammocks, blankets, and food provided some comforts to the trucker, but during inclement weather the trucker was forced to sleep under his vehicle if he was to avoid snow or rain. In some cases truckers preferred another option: lodging with some nearby farmer who earned extra money by providing room and board to stranded motorists.[27]

Operating a vehicle was a physically punishing ordeal. Solid

The aerodynamic design of this 1930 White tractor and trailer was 40 years ahead of its time. *Courtesy the White Motor Corporation.*

tires transmitted each rough spot in the road up the steering col-umn with such intensity that most drivers' hands and arms became numb after a few hours of driving. Constant effort was required to keep the truck headed on a straight course, and negotiating a sharp turn or attempting to park a truck required a great amount of physical strength. The vertical steering column was awkward and produced many aching back muscles. By 1920, improvements in steering geometry, and gearing ratios gave greater ease in steering, and these increased the stability of the front end, reducing the road shocks transmitted up the steering column.[28]

Driving comfort continued to increase as attention was given to reducing the damage to freight from vibrations caused by heavier loads. Balloon tires eased much of the road pounding, but higher quality steel, used to increase the length of leaf springs, made an

Like the wagon master, the pioneer truckers were at the mercy of the elements. *Courtesy the White Motor Corporation.*

equal contribution to riding comfort. Longer springs led to the development of the helper spring that adjusted according to the weight of the load. Leaf springs were constructed so as to have different strengths; the weaker springs provided a soft ride with reduced load, and the stronger springs would automatically come into use when the truck was carrying a heavy load. To extend the life of leaf springs and to smooth the ride yet more, shock absorbers were introduced to limit the amount of road shock on leaf springs. The driver profited, for the "bone crusher" had evolved into the "bone rattler." [29]

The early motor wagon, as the term implied, was a wagon where horsepower was replaced by motorpower. Just as the motor

Often it was courage and not engineering that enabled the long hauler to transverse the nation. *Courtesy United Van Lines.*

wagon evolved into the truck, so drivers followed a similar evolutionary process—from bullwhacker to trucker. The oldtime teamster had definitely been a member of the working class—but independent, tough minded, and spirited, and he took pride in his ability to deliver freight with little regard for weather conditions. When the bullwhacker became a truck driver, these same attitudes prevailed. Gradually the demand for drivers outstripped the supply of rugged teamsters; however, the young men who became truckers adopted many of the bullwhackers' attitudes—and were required to endure many of the same hardships. As roads were

White assembly line in 1936. *Courtesy the White Motor Corporation.*

surfaced, the truck no longer was so adversely affected by weather conditions, but the driver was. Windshields gradually became standard equipment, not so much to protect the driver from the elements as to end the blurred vision caused by the velocity of the wind striking the driver's face. Next came a roof that was an inexpensive extension of the truck body and offered some protection. The driver then added canvas side curtains attached to the roof which could be rolled down to offer yet more protection from the elements but which limited a driver's visibility.

During the 1920s manufacturers gradually adopted enclosed cabs. By the end of the decade, most production-model trucks offered some protection for the driver. Until World War II, cabs improved in quality and increased in size. The standards set by the automobile, both in design and comfort, appeared for the first time

The early Kenworth was little more than a motorized wagon. *Courtesy the Kenworth Motor Truck Company.*

on trucks during the 1930s. Adjustable padded seats, sun visors, and heaters became standard equipment. Most drivers were happy when in 1920 windshield wipers were adapted to the truck, and they were overjoyed when in the 1930s the wipers changed from hand operated to vacuum or electric powered.[30]

Moreover, advancements in smoothing out the ride made the sleeper cab practical for the first time. Many different systems were tried in order to provide the trucker a "home away from home." Some sleepers for the extra driver were located under the bed of the truck, but proved impractical. Not only was it impossible for the man in the sleeper to contact his co-worker, but also road grime thrown up by the tires penetrated the sleeper. In case of an accident there was a greater chance of the rider being seriously injured. One other unique system was tried; sleepers were placed on the side of the trailer. This system had the same drawbacks as the under-the-bed-sleeper and was soon discarded. By the late 1930s sleeper cabs for interstate drivers had developed so that a road-weary man could find some sleeping comfort. The unit was most often attached to the rear of the cab and offered a 70-inch long, 30-inch wide berth. The most popular sleeper was accessible from the cab, allowing communication with the driver while enroute, or, in the case of a lone operator, greater accessibility and avoidance of leaving the cab and braving the weather to climb into the sleeper.

Other technological improvements eliminated some of the miseries encountered on the road and reduced the accident rate. Not only was the physically abused driver tired from long hours at the wheel, making him inattentive and careless, but also he suffered accidents caused not by his error but by faulty design. Improved steering gave him greater control of his vehicle, balloon tires gave him better traction, and windshields gave him improved visibility; but the truck engineers' crowning achievement was an improved braking system. Using the early-day trucking vernacular, truck brakes were of "P and P" design: "push like hell and pray you stop." The first trucks used the same braking system as automobiles. Various methods were tried until, at the turn of the century, external contracting brake shoes replaced most braking mechanisms that locked the transmission and forced the vehicle to skid to rest.[31]

External contracting brakes used virtually the same principle as the modern system. Brake linings would contact a smooth drum that was attached to the wheel, and the friction, in theory, would stop the vehicle. An efficient braking system was slow to evolve. At first linings proved to be the major problem. Cotton and silk fabrics were tried, but failed to withstand the demands placed on them. Their replacements, leather linings, became slick with continued use and, when wet, provided little friction. In 1907 woven camel hair linings were introduced; their resistance to wear and their ability to provide adequate friction under various conditions led to the development of a woven asbestos lining.[32]

When a satisfactory lining was produced, engineers began redesigning the basic external contracting system. Several design features limited their braking power, for these brakes were exposed to water, grease, oil, and dirt that rendered their linings useless until dried or cleaned. The internal expanding system, forerunner of the modern brake, was perfected in the early 1920s. The drum and lining were enclosed to limit foreign matter from reducing the effectiveness of the brake lining. This internal system allowed for the development of servo-mechanical devices that reduced the amount of force required by the driver to stop the truck. Until 1928 improvements on the internal brake came in the form of increasing the width and thickness of the brake shoe to give increasing contact with the drum and increased longevity of the shoe.[33]

Mechanical brakes were restricted on heavy trucks because of the tremendous amount of force required by the driver to push the pedal. Therefore most heavy trucks had brakes only on the rear of the truck. However, the perfection of a four-wheel braking system allowed the introduction of hydraulic pressure systems. This new principle allowed brake pressure to be applied equally to all four wheels at the same time, thereby increasing braking power and reducing skids. The next five years proved instrumental in refining the braking system. Molded linings replaced woven; air-assisted brakes were perfected; and cast alloy brake drums were introduced to help relieve brake fading caused by expanding drums. Brake shoes and drums increased in surface area, and power brakes changed from reducing the amount of foot pressure to applying increased pressure on the drum. The metamorphosis that took place not only reduced accidents and allowed the truck to travel at higher speeds with less risk, but also reduced brake maintenance. For the 20-year period following World War I, the life expectancy of brake shoes rose from an average of 7,500 miles to 45,000 miles.[34]

A technological improvement that aided the over-the-road trucker more than it did his urban counterpart was advancement in lighting. At first trucks were equipped with the illumination used on horse-drawn wagons: kerosene lamps. These dull, glowing lanterns provided sufficient light for a teamster to travel four or five miles an hour without leaving the road, and such lanterns, hung from the rear of early trucks, reduced rear end collisions. In 1900, the R. E. Dietz Company of New York City began producing a 20-candle power, kerosene lamp that would project a beam of light up to 200 feet and promised to keep a steady flame while a vehicle traveled over rough roads.[35] The Prest-O-Lite Company, formed four years later, perfected headlights, which used pressurized acetylene gas to increase the intensity of the beam.[36]

However, progress rapidly replaced the old with the new. The electric headlight made its first appearance about 1912.[37] By 1920 most trucks were equipped with electric lights, and by the end of the decade double filament bulbs were in use. The manual hand-dimmer soon was moved to the floor of the truck, and illumination was provided for instruments on the dash. In quick succession, tail lights, side lights, and stop lights were added. During the 1930s long-haul truckers had little difficulty negotiating highways at night, and, with the addition of fog lights and high intensity bulbs in the mid-1930s, the hazards of trucking after dark were greatly reduced.

Advancements in truck design had several advantages over those made on automobiles. Whereas the car was given a new body design each year with minor mechanical improvements, truck manufacturers did not radically alter the basic structure of the truck body, but replaced outdated mechanical equipment on new models. The upshot was that owners of older model trucks could purchase the improved equipment, install it in their trucks, and gain the advantage of technologically superior service without buying new vehicles. Moreover, trucks gave better service than cars, thus increasing their longevity. Increased mileage delivered by trucks became the basic selling point used by truck manufacturers: lower cost per ton-mile. Automobiles became outdated after several years of service because new body designs with more chrome, longer fins, or bigger grills were introduced. Trucks were traded in or discarded when the cost to maintain them in good condition reduced the profits to the point where the purchase of a new model would bring greater economic rewards for the owner.[38]

Specialization within the trucking industry also led to technological improvements that otherwise would have developed more slowly. Heavy trucks were custom-made to fit hauling conditions. Dump trucks operating off the road and hauling tons of iron ore required different engines, axles, and transmissions than those on over-the-road trucks. Companies began to specialize in the building of a particular type of truck. Coal carriers, snow plows, light delivery vans, and high speed tractors all needed special

By 1940 sleeper cabs had become popular on cross-country rigs. *Courtesy the White Motor Corporation.*

equipment; major manufacturers that tried to make a standard truck to fit each job could not compete with specialty firms. Several companies were able to maintain a low-volume, high-profit business by capturing one aspect of the market.[39]

The system of specialization not only applied to truck manufacturers, but also to producers of truck parts and accessories. Most truck manufacturers at the turn of the century built their entire product out of parts they designed and constructed from raw materials. However, when as many as 500 companies failed to sell sufficient trucks to stay in business, many turned to manufacturing parts for other companies. Several of the larger components of heavy trucks cost more than a cheap automobile to produce; axles, engines, and transmissions, because of their increased complexity and costly development, ultimately were produced by but a few specialty firms.[40] Many truck manufacturers became body builders, purchasing engines, axles, transmissions, bearings, pistons, rings, and other mechanical parts from various suppliers. Ultimately the three largest automobile manufacturers—Ford, General Motors, and Dodge—dominated the light truck and standard tractor market. However, Diamond Reo, International Harvester, Mack, White, Kenworth, and Peterbilt provided the specialty, heavy-duty trucks which became the most popular among long-haul truckers.[41]

Between the major wars, firms such as White focused most of their energies on building heavy-duty trucks. *Courtesy the White Motor Corporation.*

The Company Man and the Independent Trucker

As engines increased in size, trailers became longer, and roads improved; along with the growth in strength of the Teamsters Union, working conditions for most urban truckers improved dramatically. By the late 1920s the urban driver was little different from other blue-collar workers. He toiled from sunrise to sundown for five to six days a week, usually for an hourly wage. Only on rare occasions was he required to be away from home overnight. However, conditions were different from the intercity trucker. Most often he was paid by the mile, and it was not uncommon for him to be on the road for weeks. The local hauler or hourly driver worked in order to live, but because of the mystique that engulfed the long-distance, self-employed driver, he came to live in order to work.

The stock market crash and the ensuing depression of the 1930s caused many inefficient transport companies to go bankrupt and many of the lesser skilled teamsters to become unemployed.[1] A keen competition for freight brought about even higher speeds on the road and heavier loads as those remaining in business sought to turn a profit.[2] Owner-operators had the choice of cutting rates and increasing service or remaining idle—and going out of business. Every possible expense was cut and then cut again. The owner-operator lived in his truck and would haul anything anywhere at

Truckers earning hourly wages seldom had to spend a night on the road. *Courtesy Consolidated Freightways.*

any time of day or night; he set his rates not to make a profit but only to make payments on his truck. Small businesses began using truck transportation more than ever. Low rates, an abundance of willing drivers, and speedy delivery meant that warehouse and shelf stock could be held to a minimum, thus reducing overhead costs for the businessman.

The low rates forced truckers to work longer hours and to drive more miles to remain solvent. The competition from major freighting firms, which paid low wages and charged correspondingly low rates, left truckers at the mercy of the shipper. A trucker working for an interstate firm could expect wages from five cents to a dollar an hour. The average wage earned in 1933 by interstate

In the first few decades of truckins, "we never sleep: transfer anything, anywhere" was more than an idle boast. *Courtesy the White Motor Corporation.*

drivers employed by common and private carriers was $24 for an average work week of 50 hours. However, these figures were reported by the firms and may not reflect the true earnings of employees. Also included in this survey were the wages of part-time drivers, which reduced the average number of hours that the drivers were working each week; many drivers did not work on a regular basis, but each morning appeared ready for work at the loading docks. If work was available, they would drive; if not, they would try another shipping firm.[3]

Private and common carriers required fewer hours per week of their drivers than contract or owner-operator carriers. A government survey conducted in 1933 reported that 51 percent of

This 1933 White was typical of the medium-duty, intercity rigs operating during the Depression. *Courtesy the White Motor Corporation.*

contract carriers required their drivers to drive for more than 10 continuous hours, but only 41 percent of the private carriage firms reported a like amount. Moreover, the statistics for both carriers reflected the strenuous workload required of drivers. More than 15 percent of the contract carriers reported that drivers normally were required to drive 16 hours or more each day, while private carriers reported that only 7 percent of their drivers were working similar hours.[4]

The data gathered from other than trucking firms concerning hours and wages showed a significant difference. The Association of American Railroads issued a different set of figures. Its interest was more than humanitarian; the working conditions of drivers was an important part of the railroad's argument favoring federal regulation of highway transportation. The information the railroad association reported was from data it gathered from reports made by the Delaware State Police and the Kansas Port of Entry Authority, and by observers stationed at checkpoints by these same state agencies. The association reported that the average driver earned two dollars less than the $24 per week reported by trucking firms, and wider discrepancies could be found in the remaining information. The railroad association report revealed that drivers worked an average of 99 hours each week for an average of 22.3 cents per hour.[5] The Federal Coordinator of Transportation justified the differences in the reports of the Association of Railroads and the coordinator's staff by noting the backgrounds of the drivers involved.[6] The coordinator's report was compiled from trucking firms employing drivers in urban areas, and the railroad association had gathered its data from a group of drivers hired to travel rural areas. Because "farm boys and young men from country villages" were driven to accept any form of employment under any condition rather than remain idle, the Coordinator of Transportation concluded that the data reported by the government was correct. The American Association of Railroads had been misled by the work ethic.[7]

A third set of data was compiled in the winter of 1933-1934 by various state highway patrols to provide a corresponding set of statistics for owner-operators engaged in intercity freighting.[8] One part of this compilation noted that 35 percent of the drivers contacted expected to be on the road for more than 16 hours; in that group, 22 percent estimated the duration of the trip to be longer than 24 hours. More than one-fourth of the drivers on trips of 48-hour duration had worked prior to starting the trip, but only six percent of the drivers expected no subsequent rest. However, the information gathered did not compare the amount of time a driver was behind the wheel of the vehicle with the length of time he spent waiting to unload or to load his truck.[9]

The longest hours and the most physically punishing aspect of trucking during the depression existed among that group of truckers required to endure overnight layovers. The Transportation Coordinator's survey of 1935 showed that 50 percent of the com-

"Double-bottoms" gained wide acceptance during the early 1930s. *Courtesy the White Motor Corporation.*

panies sampled in this survey provided part or all of the expenses for lodging and food for each of their drivers when they were forced to remain en route for more than one working day. A small percentage of the companies provided sleeper cabs or instructed their drivers to sleep in the truck seat. Most companies which paid for overnight expenses reserved quarters in tourist camps, hotels, or rooming houses; in some cases drivers were reimbursed for the cost of a room. Some firms solved the problem by establishing company dormitories. However, in at least one case, the dormitory was a bunk in a warehouse. An investigation by the National Code Authority in 1934 had produced approximately the same set of facts. Sixty-seven percent of the companies surveyed provided some type of sleeping accommodations; more than 60 percent were at hotels, tourist camps, or company dormitories. The remaining companies had 16 percent of the drivers in sleeper cabs, 10 percent in cab seats, and seven percent at gas stations. The drivers with sleeper cabs not only rested en route but also worked an average of 20 hours more per week while earning the same weekly salary.[10]

These surveys of trucking firms by the Federal Coordinator of Transportation did not reflect all the hardships faced by drivers. The transportation companies perhaps responded to the questionnaires with the hope of avoiding federal intervention in the trucking industry. Moreover, the coordinator believed that the companies surveyed were not representative of all the different phases of the trucking industry, and that the surveys failed to give an accurate reflection of working conditions.[11]

In the coordinator's report an addendum was appended ". . . to convey a full understanding of the rigorous exactions which are imposed on some drivers by their employers, and on others by what they conceive to be economic necessity." Such conditions were exposed by personal interviews conducted by the coordinator's field staff and by extracts from testimony before the Michigan Public Utilities Commission. The drivers involved in transporting interstate cargo, according to the addendum, worked unusually long hours of continuous service for extremely low pay. Consecutive road service in excess of 60 hours was not uncommon, and in many cases the drivers were given the choice of eating or sleeping. The employees' lack of sleep caused many to doze at the wheel. Lucky drivers hallucinated when sleep fatigue set in and would pull to the side of the road and take a short nap. Others were involved in accidents that resulted in great amounts of property damage and, in a few cases, loss of life. One embarrassed and extremely fatigued driver fell asleep at the wheel and rammed through the front of a police station. When the officers pulled him from the cab and took him into the station, the driver was so exhausted he could not sit in a chair.[12]

The monetary return for such long hours and miserable conditions was meager. One driver reported he worked for 80 hours, with three hours rest, for $12. Other owner-operators worked to pay for gasoline, meals, and payments on a truck. One owner-operator could not afford to pay his helper, but the man wanted to stay employed and worked for the price of his meals. While men

Before regulation, all that was needed to go into business was a truck and to declare that you were a "Truckman." *Courtesy the White Motor Corporation.*

became victims of the depression and cutthroat competition in transportation, others were led into the business by unscrupulous truck salesmen. Transportation brokers, for a percentage of the freight rate, would locate loads for truckers to eliminate deadheading and, as a side business, would sell trucks. Brokers promised truckers a business opportunity that could not fail. With a small down payment the trucker became an entrepreneur with monthly payments. After several months of hard work and with little return on his investment, the trucker could not make his payments. The broker then would repossess the truck and sell it to the next unsuspecting teamster.[13]

With passage of the National Industrial Recovery Act in 1933, working conditions and pay improved for many interstate drivers employed by trucking firms. A code of fair competition aimed at reducing work hours and increasing pay was instituted in 1934 for

Allied Van Lines was able to extend its operating authority by franchising its logo to independent firms. *Courtesy Southwest Transfer and Storage Company.*

the trucking industry. Drivers were allowed to work to a maximum of 108 hours in any two-week period, with overtime pay at one and one-third their normal salary for more than 48 hours worked in one week. Moreover, drivers were to be given two days off each week, and minimum wages were set according to geographical areas. However, the good intent of the federal government did not reduce the hours worked by, nor increase the wages for, the independent trucker. Not only were the regulations almost impossible to enforce, but also the owner-operator openly violated the code in order to stay in business.[14]

During the summer of 1935, Congress passed the Motor Carrier Act giving the Interstate Commerce Commission the power to regulate the trucking industry. The regulations helped reduce the working hours for many company drivers and improved the working conditions for countless others. However, many independent drivers were forced from the market place, for it was difficult to secure an Interstate Commerce Commission's certified route. If a driver could not prove that he had made regular, scheduled runs over a route prior to the passage of the Motor Carrier Act, he was denied the authority to transport goods over the route unless he could prove a public need for such a service. Most owner-operators had neither the capital nor the desire to pursue the long legal battle necessary to gain a certified route. Moreover, many small firms were able to buy out small companies, thus securing new routes and utilizing independent drivers and their equipment for a percentage of the freight rate.

Large trucking firms were able to purchase small, family-owned operations during the depression for a fraction of their worth, and with the booming wartime economy of the early 1940s the larger firms were able to afford additional capital investments. The trend has continued to the present; the approximate 26,000 firms that operated under the Interstate Commerce Commission's authority in 1940 had shrunk to approximately 15,000 by 1971. During this period of decrease in numbers of trucking firms, the amount of ton-miles carried by trucks has increased threefold.[15]

Even with the great decrease in firms, long distance trucking is not as concentrated as other transportation modes. The nation's largest carrier, Roadway Express, commands only three percent of the market. However, the firm gained its strength not from acquisition but from one of its founders, Galen Roush. During the early 1920s Galen's younger brother, Carroll, decided to quit the teaching profession and open a trucking business. He convinced Galen to give up his law practice and become his partner. Galen foresaw federal regulation of the trucking industry and established a network of routes before the Motor Carrier Act went into effect. He crisscrossed the heavily populated areas of the East with now routes. However, he had to use his training as a lawyer to fight court battles with the I.C.C. for 16 years before the company was given legal operating authority. With routes in 20 states, Roadway was able to make enough profit during the 1940s to secure more

Common carriers changed from the "haul anything, anywhere" slogans to listing the names of the towns where they could legally haul freight. *Courtesy the White Motor Corporation.*

routes by purchasing smaller firms and to expand their terminals.[16]

Other firms that did not have the cash flow nor the insight of Roadway Express management built their companies by using profits to buy routes. One such firm, Lee Way Motor Freight, started in 1934. R. W. Lee started his company with a route that included Oklahoma City, Oklahoma, and Amarillo, Borger, Pampa, and Shamrock, Texas. From this meager beginning Lee absorbed firms from surrounding states. By 1956 the firm had acquired routes to most of the major cities in Oklahoma, Texas, and Missouri and, with the purchase of St. Louis Forwarding, gained access to Chicago. For the next 10 years Lee bought an average of one firm per year, when in 1976 he had acquired a total of 21 firms. The certified routes covered 25,000 miles, cutting a wide swath across the middle of the United States bounded on the west by Southern California, on the north by Minnesota, on the east by West Virginia, and on the south by Texas.[17]

With the rise of such major freighting companies and the yearly increase in governmental regulations, independent truckers found it more difficult to make a living. However, the amount of freight hauled by trucks increased dramatically each decade, and many firms hired owner-operators to reduce capital outlay for equipment and to avoid the increased cost of union wages. Rarely did the industry suffer a labor shortage, for many drivers would rather make a marginal subsistance income owning their own truck than work by the hour driving a company rig.

The owner-operator and driver paid by the freight mile makes a living by staying on the road. If he owns his own tractor, the trucker is saddled with large payments, enormous fuel bills, and equally large sums for general maintenance. Therefore the trucker who grosses $100,000 a year, if no unusual expenses are incurred, will net approximately $20,000. But trucking is a precarious occupation. Making money depends on economy of operation and the availability of high-paying loads.

The owner who drives his own rig has several options from which to choose in seeking freight to haul. The most common arrangement is the brokerage system. Brokers obtain loads for a trucker in return for a percentage of the freight rate. Other truckers lease their equipment to a freighting company and receive a percentage of the fee that is charged the customer. Another option for the trucker is to make a contractual arrangement with a firm to haul only their goods at rates based on freight-ton-miles traveled. The most independent of the group is the "Gypsy" trucker who will "haul anything that is loose at both ends" and finds his own loads. The financial arrangements made by the trucker are not easily defined; instead of having clear-cut, black-and-white agreements between trucker and shipper, many independent truckers operate in a grey area. Frequently the commodity that is being hauled dictates the arrangement between shipper and trucker. Where special equipment is needed, greater speed required, or regular trucking schedules maintained, contractual arrangements are made.

When shipments are sporadic, seasonal, or less-than-truck-load-lots, the brokerage system or Gypsy truckers have the advantage.

The system under which the trucker makes his money becomes even more confused when he is engaged in more than one type of economic arrangement. A trucker based in Florida will carry a load of oranges to Wisconsin as a common carrier, pick up a partial load of butter under the brokerage system, and fill the rest of his trailer with packaged meat from the Chicago stockyards under a contractual agreement. The return load will be delivered to Florida and the same scheme repeated.[18]

The most structured of all systems occurs in the household moving industry. The few major firms that control the majority of household goods moved in the United States often lease tractors from owner-operators and give the owner 30 cents per mile and pay more than one dollar per 100 pounds for loading and unloading cargo; other companies pay 50 percent of the gross profits on each load. The shipping firm provides the trailer, with its name painted on the side, furniture pads, dollies, and the maintenance of the trailer. The tractor owner drives his own truck and pays for the fuel, maintenance, repairs, and labor for loading and unloading goods. The driver has to pay a minimum amount, approximately $50 for broken items and up to $300 for lost items on any single load.[19]

Interstate Commerce Commission regulations limit the number of small firms engaged in the household moving business by limiting the number of operating certificates. Thus four firms dominate the industry. Each of the major firms operates with the same basic approach in cost to customer and compensation for the trucker. The system starts to operate when an informer, who is paid as high as five percent commission for his service, relays information to a moving broker, or the person who is moving calls the local office of a moving company. The local office is manned by a broker who is paid a commission for booking the move and most often is not an employee of the moving company. Once the future customer is satisfied with a cost estimate given over the telephone, an agent will come to the customer's residence and estimate the moving cost, the day the van will pick up the load, and the day that the household effects will be delivered to their destination. All

"Bedbug haulers" often own their tractors but lease them to major firms. *Courtesy the Bekins Company.*

information gathered by the broker is then relayed to the national or regional company headquarters, and the company dispatcher determines when the truck load can be picked up. If the customer is lucky, the truck assigned to haul his household goods is on time and the broker has not overbooked the hauling capacity of the firm.[20]

"Bedbug Haulers," a trucker's vernacular for household movers, are most often victims of circumstances. If during the busy summer months they arrive two days late to pick up a load, they feel the wrath of the angry customer when it is the broker or dispatcher who is at fault. The same system applies when they are two days late to unload. Although a truck sometimes breaks down, frequently it is not the trucker's but the broker's fault for promising the customer everything in order to earn a commission. Moreover, the truck will contain more than one customer's freight, and the trucker is responsible for delivering loads according to the dispatcher's instructions. National accounts, contracts which are made with major corporations to haul their employees' household goods, usually take priority over those made with the general public, and on occasion a trucker is ordered to unload and store the cargo he has in his truck in order to pick up a national account.[21]

When the trucker arrives with the goods, the customer is required to have the cash on hand to pay for the transportation service. If he does not have sufficient funds to cover the cost, the trucker cannot unload. Often the customer is unprepared to pay the amount due because the broker has made an estimate far below the actual cost. Other times when the driver arrives at the residence, the customer is not there or it is raining, and he has to wait with no reimbursement for his lost time. If the customer is there with the money, the unloading takes place. The helpers the trucker hires to aid him in unloading the truck are not employed by the moving company agencies. Some are on call, but most are workers seeking part-time employment during summer months. The hourly rate, between three and five dollars, is a premium wage for the quality of labor that can be expected from the helpers.[22]

The trucker faces other problems of actual and alleged breakage and loss of goods which he transports. Although he inventories each piece and notes its condition, customers will argue that a table has been scratched or a box of china has been lost, when in fact the table was worn beyond repair when it was loaded and the box of china never existed. If the customer is persistent enough, the driver will have to deduct another $350 from his gross profit. However, the customer often has legitimate complaints. If the van arrives two days early, the load is stored in a warehouse and the customer is charged for storage. If a national account bumps a client's goods, delivery can run a month behind schedule. Furthermore, when household goods are inventoried before they are put on the truck, all furniture, whether new or old, is listed as being in poor condition with numerous scratches, marks, and stains. This makes it extremely difficult for a customer to get compensation for freight-damaged goods.[23]

The rates charged customers are based on various tariff schedules on a per-mile, per-one-hundred-pound freight rate. Rates vary according to city, state, region, and direction the goods will travel.

"Bull haulers" consider themselves in a class of their own. *Courtesy Marsha Holmberg.*

Consequently the rate schedules are set by different rate bureaus and become so complex that it takes a rate expert and a computer to figure out the charge. The layman has no idea how the final bill is computed and many times falls victim to a misplaced decimal point or faulty addition which cannot be detected in the final bill of lading. The regulated system also allows the unscrupulous driver, dispatcher, or trucking accountant to pad the freight bill.[24]

The total weight of the customer's household goods is determined by weighing the empty truck and subtracting this from the loaded weight. In order to cheat the system, an unscrupulous trucker first weighs the vehicle while fuel tanks are empty and he and his helpers are out of the truck. When the trailer is loaded, he stops for fuel, then has the truck re-weighed with three men in the truck. The added weight then becomes part of the load, and the customer pays extra.[25]

A load of steel headed for "Big D" (Dallas) on a tarped flatbed. *From the author's collection.*

The bedbug hauler has a unique position among truckers—he has to handle customer relations. But the other speciality haulers have their own problems. The bull hauler—a driver who hauls cattle—is in constant danger of the cattle shifting and "bunching up" to make the load uneven; thus he loses control of the trailer. Also, he has to make certain the cattle remain standing so that they will not go into shock and die. There also is the problem of loading and unloading spooky cattle and the constant odor and distasteful task of cleaning out the trailer. Steel haulers are always aware of the possibility of a load "coming loose" and the uneven load causing the rig to flip over when drivers are negotiating turns. However, for the steel hauler the greatest of all fears is a front-end collision. The inertia of the moving truck will snap the chains or bindings on the steel, and, without restraints, the steel will come crashing through the cab. The driver that pulls a flatbed—a trailer without sides—is required to "tarp" most loads. These heavy tarpaulins have to be stretched tightly over the load to prevent wind and water damage to the cargo, and they require several hours to tie, constant vigilance, and repeated tightening. When truckers are hauling by the mile, the time spent tarping is part of their free service. One trucker was disgusted when he loaded two heavy and rusted industrial laths onto his flatbed trailer and was told by the shipper they had to be tarped. On his trip from Chicago to Dallas the tarps had to be re-tied many times, on one occasion in a driving rain storm. When he unloaded the laths, the junkyard owner in Dallas told him that they could be put anywhere in an adjacent pasture.[26]

The dangerous loads truckers carry are not, as the movies would have us believe, dynamite, nitroglycerin, or munitions. Most truckers shy away from liquids, unbalanced loads, or swinging beef. The latter of the group is considered by most as possibly the worst load to carry. The beef hangs from hooks attached to the top of the trailer, and when the truck is in motion the beef sways. If the conditions of the road compel the trailer to sway or vibrate, the beef will begin swinging until the driver loses control of his truck. Some truckers also are skittish about pulling "double bottoms": tandem trailers, which are allowed in some states. These are relatively safe when traveling down interstate highways under normal conditions. However, when roads are slick from rain, when wind velocity is high, or when patches of ice and snow are scattered across bridges and shady areas of the road, hauling double bottoms can be the most dangerous of all loads. When the rear trailer starts swaying from side to side, the driver can do little corrective driving that will prevent a jackknife except slowing down and hoping for the best.

Another ever-present danger comes not from trailer cargo or equipment failure, but from hijackers. High-value loads, such as cigarettes, liquor, and copper ingots, which can have a net value of more than $200,000, are prime targets for hijackers. Moreover, other products such as television sets, radios, beef, and small appliances which are not easily identified as stolen property, are subject to the highwayman's craft. Truckers know they might be the next victim; thus they are reluctant to disclose the contents of their trailers. During the decade 1920-1930, gangsters would pull

Hauling "double-bottoms." *Courtesy the Freightliner Company.*

up to a truck, display a machine gun, and tell the driver to pull over to the side of the road. One member of the gang then would drive the truck to some remote spot where it would be unloaded. Often the driver would be blindfolded and left on a lonely road unharmed. The high incident of hijacking in Chicago in the 1920s and 1930s forced many insurance companies to cancel policies for trucks entering the area, and many truckers refused to haul freight into Chicago.[27]

Now many truckers carry pistols in their trucks and are more than willing to use them when threatened. While in large cities, truckers back their trucks up to a building so that the trailer doors cannot be opened until the truck is moved. One driver refused to haul to Chicago because he was forced to brandish his pistol to ward off three separate attempts to break into his trailer during one night, only to wake up the next morning to find that the

Trucking accidents are infrequent, but often spectacular. *Courtesy Marsha Holmberg.*

bottom of his trailer had been cut open and almost all of his load stolen. One favorite strategy of the hijackers is to wait at a stop light in an industrial section until a truck stops for the light. Then the man will jump on the step of the truck, stick his pistol in the window of the truck, and force entry.

Truckers are not immune to accepting a bribe to let themselves be hijacked, but most truckers are content to make small profits from other types of illegal and unethical activities. Some freight lends itself to an illegal exchange of goods and money. For a small bribe, a dock foreman will load an extra 100 pounds of steak on a truck which can be traded for other merchandise or can be used to bribe the company dispatcher to receive a higher-paying load. Items that are strictly regulated and have a high value take more ingenious methods of chicanery. One prime example is liquor. Every case is counted and recounted, and the driver is held responsible for any loss. Broken bottles have to be turned in with the seals intact, but the inventive trucker can salvage the expensive booze by cutting out the bottom of the bottle and draining its contents without breaking the seal. After draining most of the bottles in a case, the rest of the bottles are broken to provide proof of the alleged accident.

If the trucker is driving a company-owned rig, buys his fuel, and has his maintenance done at a friendly truckstop, he can receive up to 10 percent cash rebate on all costs, or, if he is an owner-operator, he can be given padded bills to provide income tax relief. Some truck owners illegally burn farm fuel or heating oil in their tractors to avoid paying federal road taxes. Truckers also sell and barter for stolen merchandise to add to their trucking profits without much risk of being apprehended. Often one load of illegal goods will net the trucker as much profit as six months of hard driving while hauling standard goods. The illegal cargo, ranging from "Mexican bennies" (drugs), untaxed cigarettes, and whiskey to hijacked goods, can bring as much as $20,000 to the driver who will take the risk. Some "hot" cargoes, including overweight loads and shipments for which a company does not have an Interstate Commerce Commission certificate, are low-risk hauls. Many underpaid scalemen at ports of entry will turn their heads for a few dollars.

Graft, corruption, and illegal activities should be expected to occur in an industry where union leaders are connected with the underworld and where workers falsify trip logs, admit to breaking state weight laws, and constantly break speed limits. In the trucking business, breaking the law does pay, and law enforcement is lax. Conservative estimates are that 90 percent of all long-haul truckers either keep two sets of logs to evade the not-so-watchful eye of Interstate Commerce Commission agents, or they openly violate the law by entering false information, knowing that the agents will not bother to check the authenticity. Weigh stations are avoided easily either by going around the station over back roads or by waiting for them to close. State speed laws are probably the most entertaining statutes to break and among the least enforced of all laws affecting the trucker.

Most truckers who break the law are not stealing goods, but

An independent trucker's pride and joy. *From the author's collection.*

are dodging regulations. Some drivers think that the Department of Transportation, Interstate Commerce Commission, and state transportation officials are conspiring to take away free enterprise. One tired old trucker summed it all up when he said, "Everybody on the road that is wearing a coat and tie has the authority to check your logs and fine you for having one of your lights out. It's like dealing with the Gestapo." [28]

With all the drawbacks of trucking, the owner-operators continue to complain but do not seek other employment. The reason they stay in an occupation which is becoming more regulated and more difficult to make profitable is twofold. Some truckers say it is the only skill that they have; they will not work in a union shop, and they will keep trucking until the profits decline to the point where they cannot make a living. Others give answers which will keep a future generation of social commentators reporting the romantic myth of truckers. Many are drawn to trucking for the independence that it offers; they are driven away from the monotony of the factory; they are attracted to the powerful machines; and they are lured by the opportunity to travel to distant cities. Whatever title you give it, whether it is a romantic job attachment, a search for masculinity, a symbol of the American free spirit, or the call to the open road, it keeps the trucker trucking.

Regulating the Truckers

The long-haul trucking industry developed in direct ratio with interstate highway improvements and the decline of competing rail transportation. The initial growth of the long haul came because of congested railroads, with truckers handling the overflow. However, with the return of peacetime in 1918, truckers found that less-than-carload freight shipment rates charged by railroads were sufficiently high that truck transportation could compete where parallel, hard-surfaced highway routes existed. During the 1920s railroads welcomed extended highway freight routes to provide local shipment to railheads and to transport less-than-carload short hauls. However, trucking offered speed and flexibility for door-to-door delivery which attracted first-class freight and gradually reduced rail transport of high-grade, profitable shipments.

In 1922 the Department of Agriculture submitted a report to Congress debating the relative merits of water, rail, and highway transportation and the role the federal government should assume in regulating and coordinating all phases of interstate transportation. Since 1917 motor freighting had made great advances where railroads once had enjoyed a monopoly or where new roads had been constructed, and was rapidly increasing its freight-ton-miles each year. The farmer especially had felt the influence of trucking; the average cost to haul corn, wheat, and cotton from farm to rail shipping points per ton-mile had been reduced respectively from 33, 30 and 48 cents in 1918 to 14, 15, and 18 cents by 1921. The

Milk tankers provided fresh milk to the urban areas during the Depression. *Courtesy the White Motor Corporation.*

truck had expanded the economic zone in which farmers could profitably raise cash crops, and the average haul reflected this growth; farm-to-railroad shipments in 1918 averaged a total of 11.3 miles, while in 1921 the average loaded truck haul was 47.7 miles. These averages were for all trucks traveling on Connecticut's highway system and were not an exact description of the nation-wide impact; the changing of markets varied with each agricultural zone. However, the figures reflected a marked increase in market mobility.

An indication of this change came in the corn belt. Eight hundred and thirty-one farmers who owned trucks were surveyed by the Department. Almost 25 percent had changed their markets after acquiring a truck. The average distance to market had increased from 6.9 miles to 17.6 miles; however, farmers had changed their markets after the purchase of motorized transport. According to one survey taken in the 1920s, more than 90 percent of all farmers who bought trucks gave speed-to-market as the principal advantage that trucks had over horses, while more than 50 percent reported that the greatest disadvantage of truck-to-market freighting was the poor condition of roads.

Investment in trucks followed a general trend: farmers purchasing motorized machinery to increase production following World War I. By 1920, the total number of trucks in active use on American farms numbered 139,000, a total that reached 900,000 by the end of the decade.[1]

The great increase in motor trucking by farmers had been predicted by the Department of Agriculture. Motor trucks, according to studies, would provide a valuable addition to rail transportation in farm-to-market traffic, the hauling of railroad surplus, and the transport of short hauls of less than carload lots and perishable goods. Intercity motor freighting operations would be limited to goods that required speedy door-to-door delivery and to areas where railroads could not offer competing routes. The Department based its conclusions on Connecticut's traffic census taken by a highway economist in the fall of 1921. Comparing operating costs of railroads with motor trucks per ton-mile shipments for distances from 30 miles to 243 miles, the economist thought he had found the limit for economical truck shipments. According to his conclusions, trucks could not effectively compete in the hauling of third- and fourth-class freight. However, in second-class freighting, trucks provided cheaper rates for distances up to 47 miles, in first-class up to 72 miles, and in multiples of first-class, trucks held a decided rate advantage up to 139 miles. The railroads were not able to reduce operating costs of local freight trains or overhead costs at freight depots; thus their profits declined as improved highways, funded with federal and state monies, provided a more extensive network of local, regional, and interstate routes for the trucking industry.[2]

During the 1920s highways improved, and trucking was able to attract more of the transportation dollar away from the railroads. The trend of competition between the two major transportation modes continued as the Department of Agriculture had predicted, except trucks were able to win more freight and to profit from longer hauls. As a result, motor carriers flourished.

The cost of fresh produce was greatly reduced with the use of re-frigerated trailers. *Courtesy the White Motor Corporation.*

The initial investment was low, overhead costs for small operators could be held at minimum, and many farmers trucked to provide off-season income. The trucking industry presented an economic paradox during a technological revolution; the economy of scale did not apply to this new form of freighting. Larger companies could not compete with an independent trucker because a large-scale operation could be supported only with extensive terminal and vehicle maintenance facilities. Moreover, administrative staff, dock workers, and mechanics increased operating overhead. The railroads were at a greater disadvantage when competing with an independent trucker. The railroads not only failed to compete with the shipping rates for first-class goods, but also could not provide the speed and flexibility offered by a truck.

Railroads, the mainstay of American transportation for a century, chafed under the intense competition offered by trucking. Interstate Commerce Commission regulations, setting rates for railroads, greatly reduced profits on bulk items (not hauled by truck) and kept low-volume and high-profit, first-class rates at a level at which trucks could compete. The railroad companies also reversed their traditional economic and political philosophy and argued against public subsidies for the building of roadways. Using the same arguments that had been levied against their industry at the turn of the century, railroad spokesmen agitated for reduced governmental funding for highways or for a greatly increased user tax for the maintenance and construction of roads. These increased taxes would raise highway freight rates, and the railroad would be able to compete on equal footing.

The railroad lobby found few interest groups that would support either a reduction in highway funds or an increase in user taxes. However, the attack against the injustice of regulating one mode of transportation and allowing unrestricted competition by other forms of transportation found supporters among Washington bureaucrats and large trucking firms wishing to compete by using their strongest selling point—service. The rationale for regulating the trucking industry originally was equality: either deregulate the railroads or regulate the trucks. Officials in Washington believed that, because of the nature of railroad construction, a monopoly existed and that, for the public good, rates had to be set. The trucking industry by its nature was competitive. The shipper was able to choose from among the extremes offered; large firms provided excellent and reliable service, while independent truckers specialized in low freight rates.

In 1925 the National Association of Railroad and Public Utilities, a lobby for railroads, used its political strength to get a bill introduced in Congress calling for the regulation of interstate motor freighting.[3] The bill was defeated, but was reintroduced during each of the next 10 congressional sessions until it passed. In 1926 the Interstate Commerce Commission investigated the possibility of extending its regulatory powers to include highway transportation. The Commission, after concluding its study on the economic impact of unregulated highway traffic on the railroads, determined it would not be in the best interest of the public to regulate interstate highway freight.[4]

By 1932 the Interstate Commerce Commission had altered its

During the early 1930s experienced truckers found jobs but at low wages. *Courtesy the White Motor Corporation.*

basic philosophy; it wanted to include regulating highway freight. Railroads had been attacked for price gouging and monopolistic practices, and had to be regulated for the public good. Because the same conditions did not exist in the trucking industry and because railroad lobbyists and large trucking firms were applying pressure for regulation, a new rationale for regulation surfaced: "to minimize injurious consequences by restraining competition within reasonable limits." [5] These so-called "destructive competitive practices" were a result of the general state of the American economy during the depression. The high rate of unemployment during the 1930s left many workers in the transportation field without jobs. Owner-operators in the trucking industry, faced with reduced profits, had to lower their overhead or go bankrupt. Moreover, many drivers who had been fired purchased trucks on credit and became owner-operators, and rate-cutting wars ensued. Businessmen enjoyed the lower rates. Warehouse and store stock could be held to a minimum when a fast and cheap trucking service was available.[6]

President Franklin D. Roosevelt's economic policies provided for price stabilization to ensure that established firms could make a reasonable profit in order that they might stay in business and not add to the growing number of bankruptcies. However, the cost of transporting farm commodities was held at a minimum to ensure low-cost food to the already hungry masses. Railroads suffered losses on many shipments because the Interstate Commerce Commission insisted on keeping bulk rates at a low level. Furthermore, the trucking industry had taken a large portion of the low-volume, high-profit, first-class traffic, further reducing the profits of the railroads. The Commission concluded that the motor truck had an unfair advantage; that all three major modes of transportation—water, rail, and highway—should be coordinated by regulation; and that the "existing rail and water facilities in which a large amount of permanent capital is invested should be used to the greatest possible extent. . . ."[7]

The Interstate Commerce Commission argued for authority to restrict new entries into interstate freight hauling. By reducing the duplication of service by highway carriers when other modes of freight transportation or when a trucking service was already available, destructive rate cutting could be avoided. The rationale for such regulation was the protection of the national transportation system for the public good. Investments in transportation services would ". . . deplete the revenues of other carriers, thereby weakening the financial structure of the national transportation system."[8] The Commission concluded that an excess capacity would develop in the trucking industry, resulting in intense competition, instability, and reduction of the ability of the trucking industry to respond to the public need.[9]

Congress responded to the Interstate Commerce Commission's recommendations by passing The Motor Carrier Act, which became law on August 9, 1935. The Act was later incorporated as

Part II in The Interstate Commerce Act of 1940 and contained approximately the same provisions as the original. The Interstate Commerce Commission was charged with regulating the three major classes of motor transport: common carriers available for hire on a first-come, first-served basis; contract carriers that provided specialized service for a single commodity; and private carriers that freighted privately owned goods and were not engaged in transporting property for profit.[10]

Common carriers, engaged in the most competitive phase of trucking, became the most regulated of the three classes. Minimum standards were set for employee qualifications, safety, and equipment, and maximum standards for hours that could be worked each day. Report forms and uniform accounting methods were required of common carriers to make the regulation of the large number of carriers more efficient. All interstate freighting concerns had to prove that any route and service provided was a public convenience and necessity in order to obtain the Commission's operating certificate. However, under the "grandfather clause," a firm that had provided common carrier service before June 2, 1935, and had operated until the time it applied for a certificate would receive permission to operate over the same route without proof of public need. The certificates issued would remain in force indefinitely unless the carrier violated the Interstate Act or was guilty of violation of a Commission directive.[11] Consolidations or mergers involving more than 20 trucks would have to be approved by the Commission and would be approved only if the unification was not harmful to public interest.[12]

Rates had to be published by the carrier, subject to the approval of the Commission. If these rates were considered unreasonable and discriminatory, the Commission could suspend them for a period of up to seven months and set minimum and maximum rates. Any change in rates by common carriers had to be published 30 days before they took effect. Each firm was required to insure its trucks according to the protection the Commission deemed necessary to cover loss or damage to cargo, property damage, injuries, or claims by third parties.[13]

Contract carriers were regulated under similar provisions. Permits were issued if the freighting was not against the public

Allied Van Lines was able to secure operating authority to provide national service. *Courtesy the White Motor Corporation.*

interest, but the burden of proving "public convenience and necessity" was not required. Provisions for insurance also were relaxed; liability for death or injury and for property damage other than cargo were the only restrictions. The Commission could not set maximum rates, but was authorized to set minimum rates. Furthermore, contract carriers did not have to publish their actual rates but only their minimum rates (an amendment to the Act in 1957 required contract carriers to publish their actual rates so that they would not gain unfair competitive advantages over common carriers).[14]

Regulations for not-for-hire carriers or private carriers were fewer than for the other two classes. The emphasis was not on restricting competition with other modes of transportation but on the safety of operation. Hours of driving, safety of operation, and

Federal regulation of private carriers concentrated on safety of operation. *Courtesy the White Motor Corporation.*

minimum standards for equipment came under the watchful eye of the Commission. Included under these same regulations for private carriers was the exempt class. All trucks owned and operated by farmers engaged in agricultural pursuits and not engaged in transport for hire were exempt from governmental regulations. Agricultural cooperatives, according to the legal definition of such cooperatives in the Agricultural Marketing Act, were exempt, as were all vehicles carrying livestock, shell fish, fish, agricultural commodities, and, by an amendment in 1952, horticultural products. This included all agricultural commodities that had not been processed or manufactured for resale.[15]

The Motor Carrier Act of 1935 was controversial from the

moment of its passage. Support for the act came from railroads, major trucking firms, and the Interstate Commerce Commission. Vocal attacks on the Commission's policy came from the independent truckers, transportation economists, and consumer groups. Railroads gained from the act, for the regulations artificially raised rates, limited competition, and added overhead cost to highway transportation, thus inflating highway freighting cost and putting the railroads in a more competitive position in terms of freight rates and service. Larger trucking firms supported regulation to give them an edge over independent truckers in the absence of rate competition. Furthermore, the cost of proving "public convenience and necessity," when some other trucking interest opposed the issuance of a Commission certificate, was sufficiently high to discourage small firms from entering the business. Large freighting operations and trucking organizations traditionally maintained lobbyists who protected and extended their influence in the regulation of rates, approval of mergers, and extension of routes, thereby eliminating much of the bureaucratic "red tape," expensive delays, and competition. Attorneys' fees to process appeals when certificates were refused or to fight a case which was contested often ran into the thousands of dollars; in cases where large trucking firms were attempting to establish new routes, $40,000 fees were common.[16]

Increased entry costs, special interests, and established rates reduced the numbers of owner-operators in the trucking business, but did not cause a heavy concentration of large firms. Entry into trucking was greatly restricted by regulation of the common carrier; however, the owner-operator in many cases became a contract carrier or hauled exempt cargoes. After 15 years of regulation, firms operating under common carrier certificates numbered 16,881 and freighted 50 percent of the long-haul ton miles. The largest firms, those with annual revenues of more than $200,000, which were designated Class I carriers by the Interstate Commerce Commission, collected 73 percent of the total trucking revenue. In areas where special equipment was required to transport goods, the concentration was more pronounced. The freighting of automobiles, liquid petroleum products, and household goods was controlled by a few major firms; fewer than 60 firms transported

Navajo Freight Lines has become one of the major freighters of household goods. *Courtesy Navajo Freight Lines, Incorporated.*

more than 50 percent of this freight. However, in comparison to other types of major industry, trucking has remained relatively unconcentrated.[17]

Small firms and owner-operators were placed at a competitive disadvantage not by the economics of scale but by their inability to compete with lower rates. With passage of the Motor Carrier Act came a plethora of trucking organizations, sponsored by large firms, to promote the interest of regulated highway freighting. Many of the goals attained by these organizations would be equally profitable for small firms; however, the establishment of rate bureaus, to set uniform rates for a given region, destroyed individual initiative to reduce rates according to demand and profit margin. The rate bureaus originally operated illegally in violation of the Sherman Anti-Trust Law, for their sole function was to organize a system of price fixing. Also, the government failed to prosecute the bureaus' open violation of the Interstate Commerce Act. However, in 1948, with passage of the Reed-Bulwinkle Act, the once illegal practice was sanctioned by the Commission.[18]

The Interstate Commerce Commission and members of the rate bureaus supported price fixing in order to reduce the cost of each firm printing a separate schedule of rates, to offer price stability, and to reduce open competition. The Reed-Bulwinkle amendment guaranteed that independent rate setting would not be restrained, nor would the ICC allow bureaus to set rates that were not within the interest of the general public. However, independent actions were only given a perfunctory acknowledgment by the commission and ". . . tolerated so long as it falls short of promoting genuine rate competition."[19] Rate bureaus exerted their power by dominating the setting of rates. Fees and dues paid by members of the 80 bureaus were used to promote rate changes by hiring lobbyists, printing propaganda, and challenging any independent rate proposals. Such rate changes had to be defended, and the burden of proof, as to public good, rested with the firm that made the proposal.

Rate bureaus used their extensive legal staffs and their equally extensive budgets (the Rocky Mountain Motor Tariff Bureau collected $1.7 million in 1968) to challenge most rate changes by independents. The yearly challenges against rate reductions increased from 567 in 1946 to 5,170 in 1952. Some of the requests for rate suspensions came from shippers, but more than 60 percent originated with other trucking interests. The system reduced competition by eliminating rate cuts by the independent and small-volume truckers who could not afford the legal fees to defend their position. The result has been that up to 80 percent of the contested rate changes have been withdrawn before the Commission has held its hearings.[20]

The Interstate Commerce Commission stopped so-called destructive competition between transportation modes, but at the same time freighting costs have not been reduced according to demand, nor has any real competition developed among rail, highway, and water carriers. The inherent advantage of each mode of transport has been neglected in favor of artificial rate schedules proposed by special interests groups. Truckers have had an advantage in transporting for distances up to 100 miles for most commodities, and have advantages for special classes of goods, such as perishable and household effects, for longer hauls. However, the rate structure failed to allow sufficient profits to railroads and water carriers for bulk items, thus forcing rates up on low-volume, high-cost items so that the trucking industry could compete on long hauls.[21] Moreover, low rates on natural resources and high rates on manufactured goods became an incentive for industry to locate close to urban centers instead of building plants adjacent to sources of raw material. Therefore more transportation carriers were needed, more roadway had to be constructed and maintained, and the consumer paid the cost in higher freight charges.[22]

7

Trucking Culture

Truckstops are at the center of the trucking culture. The size and service offered by the truckstops range from "mom and pop" diners that offer food and fuel to enormous, multi-million-dollar complexes. The only prerequisite to being called a truckstop is having enough room for the giant trucks to park and the facilities to dispense diesel fuel. Smaller establishments located on the two-lane, primary highway system are more abundant in Southern states. Many times the combination cafe-and-service-station is owned and operated by a single family. Much of the business is done with local truckers. However, the coffee is always strong, the food is plentiful and saturated with grease, and the building and grounds appear to have seen better times.

At the other end of the spectrum are the "Trucker Villages," "Pro-Am Truckstops," or "Trucker Centers." These elaborate truckstops offer the driver an equivalent to the cowboys' town at trails end or the friendly port to sailors. Anything a trucker needs or desires while on the road can be bought at such establishments. The only thing not available for purchase is what normally is not sought by a trucker, such as the professional services of a doctor, lawyer, or banker. But the rest is there. A trucker can get a room for the night, a shower, a haircut, a massage, a sauna, and, in some cases, a woman. For entertainment, color television is offered along with an assortment of pinball machines, pool tables, card games, and, sometimes, organized games of chance. The limit of items that

111

If there is enough space to park a large rig and have diesel fuel pumps, it is called a truckstop. *Courtesy Marsha Holmberg.*

can be purchased is almost endless: everything from a complete line of shaving gear and clothing to authentic Indian jewelry made in Hong Kong. Plastic, inflatable Mack trucks, belt buckles displaying major makes of trucks, and bumper stickers with truckers' messages are also available. The trucker buys at these shops because it is difficult for him to stop a fifty-foot tractor and trailer in a downtown area to buy day-to-day necessities, or a toy to take home to his waiting child. The old myth tourists have spread for years— "to get a good meal, eat where the truckers eat"—was more likely started by a company producing antacid tablets. The only general

Most large trucking centers offer a complete line of western clothing. *From the author's collection.*

conclusion that can be drawn by the student of truckstop cuisine is that it will be greasy. The trucker eats the same food as other customers, but in larger portions and often at a cheaper price. The main dish—either chicken-fried steak smothered in gravy, pork chops smothered in grease, or meat loaf smothered in ketchup, surrounded with mashed potatoes and a choice of one vegetable— is commonly called the daily special. The one advantage the trucker has over tourists is speedier service. The special sections set aside for truckers mean a lower booth-to-waitress ratio and a cup of coffee that neither gets a chance to become empty nor cold. By ordering the daily special the trucker can eat his meal, drink several cups of coffee, exchange a few anecdotes with other truckers, and still be back on the road in 30 minutes.

One general observation about trucking culture is that all major truckstops have the same motif. Each restaurant is sterile.

Service is fast but would not appeal to the discriminating palate. *From the author's collection.*

The countertops are Formica, the booths are vinyl, the floors are terrazzo, and the rest is stainless steel and glass. Attempts to decorate with plastic flowers, western prints from dime stores, Spanish paintings on velvet, or cute milk dispensers in the shape of a cow add to the starkness. Truckers are not looking for elegant surroundings, but they do demand one element to appeal to their aesthetic senses—a jukebox. Two things are for certain at a truckstop: the waitress will always be pouring coffee and the jukebox will always be belting out country and western music.

If the restaurant is not crowded and the jukebox is silent, a waitress will request that a trucker put money in the machine and play her favorite song. At other times a more gregarious waitress will use her tip money "to match" the trucker to decide who will fund the noise machine. It goes without saying that trucker songs receive the most requests.

"For Professional Drivers Only" sections are marked at major truckstops. *From the author's collection.*

June "Barbie Doll" Baker, waitress working in the truckers' section. *From the author's collection.*

Employees at truck stops take on the attributes generally identified with the drivers. Smiles are rare. Waitresses appear on the verge of being friendly, but they always keep an aloofness between them and drivers for fear some driver might mistake friendliness for sexual advances. Drivers flirt with the waitress as if it is required; therefore, the older and more efficient waitresses work the section marked "for truckers only." After years of waiting on tables, these women have heard every "come on," and by repetition they have become experts in quick retorts. The natural look that has become popular among American women as a result of the youth movement has not made its impact on women in roadside restaurants. Their styles belong to the 1950s except for the shortened length of their pastel or white—and slightly soiled—uniforms. Heavy and bold makeup combined with bright red lipstick add to the surrealistic appearance of their permanently stacked, sprayed,

Gloria "Dark Eyes" Michel recently wedded her boss in the Transport for Christ sanctuary. *From the author's collection.*

and often bleached hair. They are cool, efficient, and impersonal, a mixture that blends well with the neon and plastic of the truckstop.

Providing personal services for drivers is not where a truckstop gains most of its profit. The extras, including rooms, food, and entertainment, are to lure truckers in from the road to the fuel pumps or service area. It is easy for a trucker to spend three hundred dollars for fuel and maintenance during a single stop, and excellent personal service results in repeat business. At large truckstops more than 1,000,000 gallons of fuel will be sold each month to more than 20,000 truckers. In an effort to attract repeat business, managers of these stations provide many things. As one manager stated, "What the trucker wants, the trucker gets."[1]

One aspect of the workingman's culture is missing from the truckstop: alcohol. Drivers who will not resist taking pills to stay awake on long trips will abstain from consuming any alcoholic bev-

Reverend Paul Phillips' 18-wheeled Transport for Christ mission. *From the author's collection.*

erages. Many truckers admit to drinking heavily while off duty, but they consider drinking and driving a taboo of their occupation.[2] However, other forms of special entertainment are available to the trucker, some from business establishments located close to the truckstop (often owned by the same individual) and others available in the truck parking lot.

Traveling gospel shows, housed in semi-trailers, provide Sunday services conducted in truckers' language. While denouncing the sins and evils of governmental regulation, pills, and prostitutes, these preachers promise fire and brimstone for sinners in a manner reminiscent of the tent evangelists of fundamental sects during the 1950s—or 1920s. The mixed metaphors used to sway drivers to "take Christ into their hearts" appear to have been garnered from some country and western song which failed to make the charts. Highway evangelists are not new to trucking, but only in recent

"Highballing to Winnemucca," a hand-painted, electrified oil for $39.95 (extension cord not included). *From the author's collection.*

years have they attracted a sufficient following to expand their operations. One evangelist has a fleet of trucks, allowing him and his fellow ministers to deliver the gospel at truckstops across the nation. The most famous minister trying to convert truckers is Jimmy Snow of Nashville, Tennessee. The son of country and western star Hank Snow, Reverend Snow, besides saving the souls of truckers, produces a religious program at the Grand Ol' Opry. Although the main thrust of his religious instruction is aimed at the country and western stars of Nashville, Reverend Snow attempts to reach truckers through the use of citizen band radio.[3]

The fundamental and decidedly southern religious instruction given to truckers is evident at truckstops' gadget shops. Rhinestone studded crosses, plastic replicas of Jesus, and paintings of Christ leading a truck to safety adorn many gift shop walls. Chapels, constructed at many truckstops, display paste-on stained glass windows and provide an additional religious stimulus to bring the wayward driver back to the fold.[4]

For truckers who have not given up their sinful ways, as well as for those trying to walk the straight and narrow, truckstops offer many secular temptations. The parking area where the churches on wheels park to fill their pews also contains roving prostitutes in vans and mobile homes selling their wares. These working girls go from truck to truck asking the driver if he wants to "have a good time." With the aid of CB radio, this appeal can now be made over the airwaves. Prostitutes, although not present at all truckstop parking lots, sometimes are housed in brothels located adjacent to larger truckstops. In the small towns of Nevada, where prostitution is legal, truckers constitute a large percentage of the patronage at houses in red light districts.[5]

If the trucker is interested in looking instead of buying, a wide range of topless, bottomless, and even all-nude truckstops await his attention along the interstate.[6] Truckers Valley, located seven miles east of Wheeling, West Virginia, is a prime example of what is offered the trucker as he travels across the nation. The Windmill Truckers' Center, one of three truckstops on the Dallas-Pike exit of Interstate 70, typifies the large truckstop. The multi-million-dollar business is a trucker's shopping center and more. The owner, Lee Glasnor, estimates that 484,000 truckers each year buy 30,000,000 gallons of fuel from him; to maintain this average, more than 400 trucks have to visit his establishment each 24-hour period.[7]

The side attractions in Truckers Valley fill most of the drivers' needs and desires that cannot be satisfied with food and fuel. For the literary enthusiast, there is an adult book store offering a wide range of pocket books and magazines to be purchased, read, and then tucked away in the glove compartment. For those who want the same stimulation but prefer a different media, an adult movie theater with double-features is available. For remaining truckers not inclined to spend their money on photographs, racy novels, or celluloid, the Lucky Lady Lounge features erotic dancers to stir their imagination. The Lucky Lady, like most establishments in states where whiskey cannot be sold by the drink, is a private club. However, the first visit is free when a two-dollar membership card is bought—which happens to be the admission charge for card-carrying members. West Virginia's laws prohibit dancers from appearing in the nude, so the dancers usually wear at least a gold chain around their waists. For drivers who wish to rest, two motels provide rooms, and for truckers worried about their physical well-being the "King of the Road Health Club" replenishes their tired, aching bodies and fulfills some of their fantasies through massage.[8]

A social hierarchy and class consciousness has developed at these highway cultural centers. At the base of such rankings is physical appearance, both of dress and personal style. Cowboy attire of the modern variety—lizard boots, Levi jeans, sculptured leather belts, giant shiny buckles, plaid shirts (always long sleeve, but the wearer is allowed to double roll them to three-quarter length or even up to and past the elbow), an occasional cowboy hat—has become the socially accepted uniform of the truck driver. Although some aberration can be found among truckers, most will wear enough of the accepted clothing to withstand the critical judgment of their peers. On rare occasions older truckers who have survived the rigors of trucking for 20 years can be seen in truckstops dressed in khaki pants and shirts with a soiled Stetson hat cocked on their heads. Moreover, young people of the late 1960s and early 1970s who have entered trucking have brought with them the unorthodox style of the counter culture and have affected new dress codes. More truckers are sprouting beards, adorning themselves with jewelry, and displaying patches on their denim clothing.

Hair styles range from the clean look of the 1950s, including flattops, burrs, and Princetons, to the Elvis Presley, ducktail-in-the-back and greasy-curl-in-the-front look. The average driver cares little for the styled, razor cut, fluff-dried look popular among the college age generation; instead he lets his hair grow over the tops of his ears, his sideburns below the bottom of his ears, and, in the back, his hair will often touch his collar. The men's hairspray industry has found few customers at truckstops; the old commercial that "a little dab will do you" appears to have made its impact on most drivers. Some would conclude that the pragmatic trucker has realized that if one dab works well, two dabs will do wonders.

The second most noticeable attribute of truckers who rank high on the social scale is personal style. They swagger from truck

Independent trucker John "Paleface" Baker started trucking during the 1960s. *From the author's collection.*

Truckers grabbing a quick cup of "100 mile" coffee. *From the author's collection.*

to restaurant. As they mount a vinyl, rotating stool at the counter, they assume a casual, almost slouched, posture while drinking coffee, and they conduct gentle flirtations with the waitress. All these require large amounts of tactfully displayed masculinity. The trucker has to maintain a nonchalant attitude and temper his actions as well as dress so as not to draw undue attention. The greenhorn, resembling the historical "city dude" in the West, often exaggerates his walk, wears brightly colored western shirts, or talks too loudly. It is easy to spot the young man not yet totally acquainted with truck-driving culture as he timidly sits in the section marked for truckers only and nervously glances from side to side, looking for approval.

The restrictions placed on the driver's actions and dress do not apply to his most prized possession: the command of a diesel powered tractor. Design, be it cab-over (the cab placed directly over the

A cab-over Kenworth tractor. *Courtesy the Kenworth Motor Truck Company.*

engine to reduce the total length of the tractor) or a conventional configuration, makes little difference. Drivers have personal preferences on design, for each has distinct merit. The shorter, cab-over rig allows the driver to pull longer trailers, provides greater visibility, a shorter turning radius, and easier access to the engine. However, the cab arrangement puts the driver closer to the engine which results in more interior noise and vibration. The conventional cab arrangement, with the engine in front of the cab, provides greater protection in case of an accident, and the weight of the engine at the front of the vehicle provides a smoother ride by reducing the buckling effect of the trailer. Also the longer wheelbase on the conventional cab enables the vibrations encountered

A conventional Kenworth tractor. *Courtesy the Kenworth Motor Truck Company.*

from a rough spot on the road to be muffled by the front suspension before the rear wheels come in contact with the same irregularity.[9]

The two types of tractors are equipped with the same engines, transmission, and accessories. But the conventional tractor, with its long, lacquered hood and massive chrome grill, inspires awe not only in most mortals who drive automobiles but also in most truckers. Of the top-of-the-line models, Kenworth conventionals are considered the best, and drivers of the so-called "K-Whoppers" are the most envied. Drivers of these expensive and powerful rigs take great pride in selecting the right interiors, custom paint jobs, and chrome fixtures.

In his daily routine of fulfilling the role of a trucker, the driver is confined in action and dress, but in adorning his truck there is no

Inside of cab-over Transtar II. *Courtesy International Trucks.*

limit. As one trucker put it, "I spent more time selecting my truck than I did in picking out my old lady." These personal touches in accessories cover a wide spectrum of practical items mixed with gaudy displays of conspicuous consumption. The accessories that can be purchased for a truck include all those sold by the manufacturers—and many more. Seats with adjustable mechanical and air shock absorbers smooth out the jarring ride, while the feel of Naugahyde provides added comfort and aesthetic value. Electronic conveniences abound: citizen band radio, quadrophonic stereo, AM-FM radio and tape player, and radar detector, while an instrument panel that appears to be copied from a Boeing 747 graces the firewall. Shag carpeting and custom console give the driver some of the comforts of home, and, with the extra-wide and long sleepers measuring three feet by eight feet, the driver can bed down in comfort. The cost is $3,000 above what the average American paid for a new house in 1975. With an investment of $45,000, the owner-operator thus takes to the road hoping that he can log enough miles to make his payments.[10]

The tractor plays an important part in the trucker's life. His sense of personal identity, masculinity, power, and pride thereby is displayed for other truckers. Moreover, the tractor provides him his sole source of income and, at the same time, becomes a home. It is no wonder that a trucker wants to add personal touches: his mother's name on the fender, flames scalloped from the grill back across the hood, or his handle (his nickname or name he uses on the CB) printed in perfect detail on the doors. The design and color scheme painted on trucks are not haphazardly chosen, but are a result of many hours of planning and dreaming. Truck manufacturing companies realize the importance of personalized rigs and offer a wide range of options to persuade drivers to buy their product.

Kenworth, one of the top custom truck builders in the world, offers optional equipment that will fit almost any need. Its self-proclaimed and often repeated title, "Rolls Royce" of trucks, connotes engineering excellence and a range of options, but after viewing the price tag an argument could be made that the title refers to an economic class. Kenworth had made its reputation by building a top-quality, lightweight body and offering a long list of proven, name-brand engines, transmissions, fifth wheels, and axles as optional equipment. The company does make trucks that have standard equipment. A typical example is the W-900 series. A cab, constructed of aluminum and fiberglass, a frame built with die-quenched steel, and a fuel tank molded from aluminum are made by the Kenworth Company, as are the suspension, heater, electrical and cooling systems. However, the front and rear axles are made by Rockwell, the alternator by Motorola, the engine by Cummins, and the transmission by Fuller.[11]

The optional equipment list, including equipment made by Kenworth, provides replacements for almost all parts. The Rockwell axles can be replaced with Eaton's equivalent, the Motorola alternator can be replaced with a Delco-Remy, and the Fuller transmission can be replaced by any of the 38 other transmission models offered. The standard six-cylinder, 855 cubic inch, 290-horsepower Cummins engine could fall victim to one of the four Caterpillar, six Detroit Diesel, or 11 other Cummins engine models that appear on the options list. The most powerful and most sought after is the 12-cylinder, 456 horsepower Detroit Diesel.[12] Cummins builds a competitive 450-horsepower plant, and in the race for bigger and more powerful engines Cummins has developed and is now testing the KT600—with a rating of 600 horsepower.

After selecting the drive train that will move the truck down the road at a pace and the ease he desires, the trucker selects the style in which he wants to travel. Again, specialty companies stress personalized, custom, made-to-order trucks catering to the independent nature of each driver. Truckers pay as much attention to the outside appearance of their trucks as they do to the mechanical options, and truck companies extend themselves to provide a variety. Kenworth Truck Company's paint brochure offers suggestions for "paint schemes," and promises, "We won't give you any of this one-design, three-colors-to-choose-from business!"[13] Future customers are invited to look at company designs, but at the same time the firm is prepared to use any of the hundreds of paint colors available to produce a personal design created by the trucker.[14]

The cab-over-engine models with a sleeper attachment have 14 company designs with suggested colors. The names given each design have been borrowed from famous and often historical towns of the Northeast, where the short tractor is necessary because the maximum length laws in that region are shorter than the national average. Bostonian, Lexington, Yorktown, Georgetown, Salem, and Monticello are neither part of a roll call of place names of the American Revolution nor of Kenworth's contribution to the Bicentennial celebration, but rather are design patterns on a few of their cab-over-engine-trucks. Conventional trucks have similar regional connotations attached to design models. However, the conventional is a Midwestern and Western truck, and the names imply open spaces, majestic places, and frontier heritage. The West Coast trucker can select from the Sequoia, Olympic, Willamette, Columbia, Rainier, Yosemite, or Shasta models. The trucker that identifies with the Midwest or Southwest also has a wide selection: Big

Horn, Carlsbad, Rio Grande, Dakota, Laramie, and Aztec. The Southern driver can also feel at home with the Blue Ridge, Ozark, or Dixie models.[15]

If the trucker is interested in other accessories, these are available: fog lights, flood lights, red lights, amber lights, air horns, dual exhaust pipes, and "as much chrome and stainless steel as you want."[16] For driver comfort and safety, an auxiliary defroster fan, air conditioner, outside sun visor, powered window lift, or chrome mirror with a heating element can be installed.[17]

The only luxury item that most truckers will not purchase is an automatic transmission. The skill involved in shifting 20 gears to maintain maximum speed and power not only requires the driver to listen to the engine and read a tachometer (which registers the revolutions per minute of the engine), but also gives him a feeling of control and power. An automatic transmission with seven forward gears is almost as efficient, but is much more effeminate. The cost of an automatic transmission above a manual model also is sufficiently high to lower demand. Therefore most sales of such transmissions are to companies engaged in overseas trucking operations where the natives have had little training in the skills necessary to shift 20 gears. Purchasing agents for major firms realize that the $6,000 invested in an automatic transmission will reduce accidents and lower the total amount of time it takes to train foreign truck drivers.[18]

Yet the most impressive feature of the modern truck is the interior of the cab. The "ultra-luxury and handsome appointments" that grace the sleeper provide a "bedroom on wheels." The Kenworth top-of-the-line luxury package is the V.I.T. (Very Important Truck). With "the prestige of a thoroughbred, and the comfort of a Rolls Royce," the trucker is offered the ultimate in luxury, convenience, comfort, and prestige which, says one ad, he has "worked so hard to achieve." The sleeper lives up to the trucker's expectations; the bed holds a normal size, twin mattress in the conventional truck and has an optional full-sized mattress in cab-over models. The eight-foot-wide, five-foot-deep sleeper is lined with "luxurious diamond-tuffed upholstery with accent buttons." Included within the sleeper is a 12-volt cigar lighter, a full-size closet with separate light, and two shelves for books, shaving kit, or

The top-of-the-line Kenworth Vista Cruiser. *Courtesy the Kenworth Motor Truck Company.*

portable television. For convenience, there are controls separate from the rest of the cab for the heater, air conditioner, radio speakers, and interior lights mounted next to the bed.[19]

Although the V.I.T. sleeper looks like a playboy pad rather than the inside of a truck, Kenworth, in honor of the American Revolution—and in order to sell more trucks to husband-wife trucking teams—has produced a limited number of "V.I.T.-200, Bicentennial Kenworths." The cab in these offers all of the luxury items of the average V.I.T. plus a taller sleeper with vista cruiser windows, electrical hookups for 110 volts of alternating current, and a chemical toilet, which the salesman promises will not splash, spill, or stink. And, of course, the Bicentennial seal adorns the truck body, which is basic white with red and blue trim.

Such expensive rigs most often are purchased by owner-operators, but the trend is changing. Fleet owners report that the more expensive trucks attract better drivers, that truckers will perform more mechanical, washing, and polishing duties, and that they generally take better care of a new, shiny, luxury vehicle. Moreover, drivers take pride in working for a company that buys better equipment, thus reducing the employee turnover rate and loss due to freight and tractor damage.

The giant tractors represent $50,000 of chrome and stainless steel, of fiberglass and aluminum, of iron and vinyl. They are more than symbols of the power, sex, speed, and free spirit that Americans have attached to the motor vehicle. They are more than the myths associated with the transporters of goods. They are the self-expressions of men who are independent, displaying their frontier pride in being a part of a romantic occupation.

The popular conception of a trucker as a large, slow-moving, dullwitted, muscular, tattooed man with greasy clothes and un-shined army boots would no doubt describe a small minority of modern truckers. However, data collected by psychologists administering physical and psychological tests to truckers produces a different image. Truckers, as a group, conform to the average height and weight of the American population in general—and test above average in intelligence. Over-the-road drivers did score below average on artistic appreciation and musical aptitude.[20] One obvious reason for the popular belief that truckers were of less than average intelligence was their anti-social behavior toward people outside their profession. Furthermore, truckers spent most of their day on the road alone at the wheel; when social intercourse became available, variety and intellectual stimulation often was lacking in their conversation. The lonely hours behind the wheel, traveling unbroken interstate highways, left the trucker a man of few words. Moreover, only in the last few years has the noise level in trucks been reduced to the point where conversations or radios can be heard above engine noise.

Even with the AM-FM stereo tape deck belting out "Johnny

Cash and all that trash,"[21] or the constant chatter on the CB, long-haul drivers have had to resort to mental games to keep their minds occupied. A favorite pastime among truckers is daydreaming; recalling old experiences and visualizing future plans. During the long hours on the road with the roar of the engine as sole companion, the trucker became an expert at conjuring up mental images. Past experiences, both pleasant and unpleasant, were relived, and the emotions attached to each memory was retasted. One old trucker admitted to being a "qualified expert on daydreaming"[22] after trucking for more than 30 years. He had acquired the habit of remembering dates, names, and encounters on the road. When driving at night, he would relive all the important memories of his past. As the hour of the day, day of the week, day of the month, and year of each important event in his life rolled from the tip of his tongue, his eyes twinkled with each pleasant adventure, and he became angry with each account of tickets he had received.[23]

Daydreaming on the road is limited only by a trucker's creativity and covers a wide spectrum of subjects. A majority of truckers over 50 reflect on past glories or look toward retirement. The 35-to-50-year-old group are prone to plan vacation time, work around the house, or activities with their families. In one such case, a driver committed house plans to memory, building one home, then the next, and was contemplating his third house. Younger drivers think of future good times at a special truck stop, of visiting girlfriends or wives, or of how they will finance the expensive truck of their dreams. Tapedecks and radios have eliminated some daydreaming among truckers, but new electronic gadgets soon become boring on long trips, and truckers shut out the static and everpresent country music; with the flip of a switch they can return to the age-old art of daydreaming.

Closely associated with the mental activity of daydreaming is the condition of hypnagogic hallucination. The phenomenon occurs during the stage between sleep and wakefulness. Among truckers this condition is brought about by operational fatigue, compounded by insufficient sleep and the mesmerizing effect of traveling a long stretch of uninterrupted road. In a majority of cases, drivers report that the hypnagogic phenomenon occurs while they are driving on a long-distance run during darkness and

"Old Prospector" napping between truck repairs. *Courtesy Marsha Holmberg.*

are "fighting to stay awake."[24] The hallucinated object appears suddenly on the roadway, and the driver has to make an emergency stop to avoid hitting the object. The driver does not realize that he is suffering an hallucination until the vehicle has stopped; even then, some drivers will refuse to believe that the object did not exist.[25]

The hypnagogic phenomena are often influenced by the conditions that the driver has encountered during the day. One driver carrying a load of hogs to the stockyards, a task he thought unpleasant, was driving a long, seldom-traveled section of flat roadway when a giant, pink hog appeared in the road. After skidding to a halt to avoid hitting the animal, the driver awoke to find the road empty except for black smoke coming from his tires.[26] Cattle and deer crossing signs often trigger hallucinated animals. One driver reported seeing logs laid across the road the night after some Teamsters threatened to halt all independent trucking by felling trees across the highways. Most truckers who push their bodies beyond their physical limits experience the phenomena, and a few have accidents as a result of emergency stops. When all the brakes on a truck are locked to avoid hitting an hallucinated object, the trailer skids out of control and the rig turns over.[27]

Somewhere between daydreams and hallucinations is yet another condition that effects most truckers: memory deception. Drivers on a long haul are social recluses and, when alone, daydream about the most exciting event that happened to them or that they wish would happen to them. After the daydream has been repeated thousands of times, it becomes increasingly hard for the trucker to distinguish between daydream and reality. Exciting stories circulate in endless repetition at truckstops, and truckers are happy to repeat an entertaining yarn as a personal experience. Evading speed traps, making record-breaking trips from coast to coast, or (the old standby) picking up a young, attractive female hitchhiker clad only in a raincoat, have become favorite stories of truckers. These men admit that other truckers repeat the same adventure yarn year after year, but each time the event becomes more exciting—and each time the trucker will swear it is the truth.

The physical and mental demands placed on drivers to meet financial obligations and job requirements often are beyond human endurance. Moreover, some drivers use what little vacation time or days off they might receive to "live it up." Drivers spend their free time seeking the pleasures of life not afforded on the road; often they return to duty more exhausted than when they left. The result is that some form of stimulus is consumed by many—perhaps a majority of—long haulers to enable them to stay on the road. Gallons of strong "hundred-mile coffee" are consumed by truckers for the caffeine content. Chain smokers, tobacco chewers, and tea drinkers seeking a mental uplift abound in the trucking industry.[28]

However, stimulation is not confined only to those retail products that the general public uses to stay alert. "West Coast Turn-Arounds," "Reds" and "White Crosses" have become part of the attraction of the truck stop. The pills are labeled according to their strength, effect, or the particular drug contained in each. Most of these illegal, prescription drugs available to the trucker are generally described as "bennies." This short title for benzedrine connotes the popularity of the drug and its general availability.[29] Benzedrine, discovered and dubbed "speed" by the counter culture in the 1960s, stimulates the central nervous system. The effect of the drug varies with each individual, but in general the body functions increase in efficiency. Small amounts of the drug will alleviate and often reverse conditions caused by fatigue.[30]

Truckers take benzedrine to increase the hours they can spend behind the wheel, but often the drug does not perform that function. With larger doses, a person under the influence of bennies may become euphoric, thus taking unnecessary risks but feeling immune to accident. Other side effects include irritability, loss of concentration, and, with long term use, teeth will decay. Moreover, in some cases benzedrine has no effect. Yet when it does provide increased alertness, the effect often disappears with little warning to the user. When the driver ceases taking the drug, or "comes down," he often suffers a severe hangover much like the condition associated with the excessive intake of alcohol. Headaches, muscle cramps, depression, and fatigue usually follow; the period of time necessary for a driver to recover without the aid of yet more drugs extends beyond the normal rest period needed to overcome the fatigue of extended hours of work.[31]

The availability of pills at the truckstop and their use by drivers are major concerns of many over-the-road drivers. "Pill heads" generally are considered dangerous and are social outcasts. Moreover, drivers report many cases of hypnagogic phenomena occurring with greater frequency among those who take drugs. One driver questioned about the use of drugs in the industry reported that he had been involved in an accident because of his co-driver's dependency on pills. He had been driving through an isolated farming section in Nebraska, became tired, and asked his co-driver to relieve him. The other driver took a couple of "White Crosses"—about ten grams of benzedrine—and assumed control of the truck while the first driver climbed into the sleeper. A few hours later he awoke to find his co-driver in the sleeper with him and the loaded truck traveling about 50 miles an hour across a wheat field. After the truck came to rest, axle deep in mud, the first driver asked his replacement what had happened. His response was, "Bennie said he would take over, so I gave him the wheel."[32]

The loss of sleep leaves its mark on long haulers. The one distinguishing feature of all truckers, according to the United States Health Service, is injection and inflammation of the conjunctiva—or, in layman's terms, bloodshot eyes. However, drivers complain of indigestion, constipation, diarrhea, kidney ailments, backaches, hemorrhoid problems, and loss of hearing. One occupational hazard difficult to measure is the rapid aging of men who have engaged in trucking for a period exceeding five years. The deep lines that normally appear on a man's face at age 60 can be found on truckers 20 years younger.[33] In recent years, profits have decreased, red-tape has compounded, and speed limits have been lowered, but the trucker continues to abuse his body as he travels across the nation in search of a high-paying load.

The reasons why men choose to truck are as varied as those explaining why any skilled laborer selects an occupation, except for one important criterion—independence. From the moment the engine of a big rig is cranked and the transmission is engaged, the trucker is his own boss. Coffee breaks, the end of a work day, and time for lunch are neither determined by a factory whistle nor by a time clock; when the driver "damn well pleases," he pulls his rig into a truckstop. Along with this independence comes a high degree of responsibility. A $60,000 piece of machinery with a $200,000 payload gives the trucker a sense of immense responsibility and power. Some truckers say the job pays more money than they could make in another occupation, but others proclaim that the salary is not important. Many have quit trucking to take a "regular" job, only to be drawn back by the lure of the open road or by the sound of a big diesel rolling on a distant highway.

And truckers are lured into the business by the large sums of money that can be made by an owner-operator. The myth that all truckers make small fortunes continues to survive, but many variables are involved in making a profit. Most of these so-called small fortunes, when all expenses are deducted from the trucker's gross income, actually are close to the average skilled worker's wage. Another factor often overlooked is long hours of service. When truckers boast of annual net incomes of more than $20,000, they probably have worked in excess of seventy hours per week with little or no time off. A union carpenter or plumber employed in an industrialized state in the Northeast, working the same hours but taking two weeks' paid vacation each year and enjoying other benefits not given the trucker (health insurance, pensions, and sick leave), would make in excess of $40,000.

When asked why they stay in trucking, drivers who are happy with their occupation respond with one worn-out phrase, "It gets in your blood." On the few days that they are home or have been forced to stop for repairs, truckers get itchy feet and cannot wait to get back on the road. The drivers exhibit an unrestrained optimism in moving up the economic and social ladder with a new, bigger, and more powerful truck. A few highway entrepreneurs look forward to buying an additional truck, hiring a driver for the rig, and hopefully one day becoming the owner of a small fleet. A few have succeeded, but most hope only for lower fuel prices, an expanded interstate highway system, a more expensive truck, and some end to the myriad state and federal regulations—and regulators—who plague their existence.

Electronic Folklore

Before the popularization of the citizens band radio, modern day trucking was an obscure occupation. The general public had little knowledge about the trucker's day-to-day life, and mass media did little to exploit this mute hero. Most travelers on the nation's highways had few reasons to talk to truckers and only occasionally saw them at truckstops, eating at separate dining sections. Travelwise motorists often would ask trucker's advice on the best routes to take, road conditions, or locations of possible speed traps. The only other form of communication came on the road with various light and hand signals. During these exchanges the trucker was considered the expert and the motorist the amateur. Verbal communication was often brief and curt. Therefore, one of the most important aspects of a popular folk hero was missing—his language.

Before the rich and colorful syntax of the trucker became common knowledge, the long hauler was identified with a larger grouping of blue-collar workers. Lumbermen, steeplejacks, and merchant marines have the physical attributes and independent qualities which made them folk heroes, but like the trucker, their occupations were more symbolic than real. The opportunity for a child living in a small Midwestern town to view a ship docking at sunset, a steeplejack silhouetted against a pale blue sky, or a lumberman striking his last blow with an axe was confined to his imagination. These same obstacles kept adults from feeling the salt spray, hearing "timber" and the crashing of limbs echoing through the mountains, or experiencing the exhilarating challenge of walking a beam high above the pavement. However, truckers do that which most of us do—they drive—they drive more miles, drive bigger vehicles, and drive for a living, but everyone who drives experiences the power, the independence, and the longing to travel the open road. Because most Americans can neither give up a house in suburbia nor leave the security of their jobs, they vicariously experience the trucker's freedom of mobility through the citizens band radio.

Although CB sets have been available to the general public since the issuance of the first license in 1947, most individuals had little use for the expensive and exotic equipment. A Federal Communications Commission license charge of $20, discouraged some, and the first ultra-high frequency channels set aside, limiting operating range to short distances, discouraged others. Moreover, the equipment was complicated to use, bulky, and expensive. In 1958 the FCC opened up a new, lower frequency band with 23 channels, which gave citizens band radios a more effective range.[1] Along with the improvement made by FCC came the discovery of the transistor and import of inexpensive Japanese CB units. However, these efforts by the government and Japanese industry would have gone unnoticed by most, if it had not been for fuel shortages and the timely truckers' slowdown and strike.

During December of 1973 the Arab oil embargo produced long lines at gasoline stations, and what fuel that was available sold at a premium. President Richard Nixon's solution to the impending fuel crisis was to conserve as much fuel as possible in order to ward off rationing. Truckers faced long lines at the fuel pump, and the price of diesel fuel rose from 27 cents per gallon to more than 50 cents per gallon.[2] Most drivers already had developed a long-standing hatred for federal regulations and blamed bumbling bureaucracy for high fuel prices. On December 3, 1973, over the protest of most truckers, Congress voted to establish a uniform 55 mile per hour speed limit on the nation's highways.[3] Truckers that were paid by the mile or a percentage of the gross profit each trip denied the claim that the reduced speed would save fuel. Moreover, the speed limit reduction increased the amount of hours they would have to drive in order to maintain their standard of living. The combination of a federally imposed speed limit and the ever-escalating fuel prices was seen by the truckers as a vendetta by the federal government to stifle free enterprise.

The independent trucker's appeal to the federal government to reinstate speed limits and to lower fuel prices fell on deaf ears—and a nationwide independent truckers' strike ensued. Truckers across the nation sharing a common goal—deregulation—united in protest. National media coverage of the wildcat strike, truck convoys, and associated violence stirred some public sentiment, but far more significant was the coverage of CB usage. When the truckers organized the airwaves, using the CB to orchestrate the movement of trucks, the news media broadcasted the colorful CB lingo to a receptive audience.

Many people throughout the nation did not want to drive only 55 miles per hour—for any reason, including gasoline conservation. Thus trucker and non-trucker were united. Their common enemy was not the federal government but a representative of governmental authority, "Smokey". Almost overnight drivers believed they needed a CB to maintain vigilance on the road. From 1959 to 1975 the FCC only had issued one million licenses to CBers. When the demand for radios was recognized by industry, sets not only became more sophisticated but also cheaper. The new gadget rapidly changed from a luxury item to a necessity for average American travelers. This seemingly insatiable demand can be illustrated by the issuance of more than one million licenses in 1976,[4] and by the spring of 1977 an estimated 10 million sets were transmitting.

Americans eagerly bought CBs. When asked why they had bought a set for their automobile, the usual reasons were practical, and the CB does have a practical side: being able to call for help when stranded on the highway, inquiring about road conditions, or reporting accidents. However, the attraction is more than pragmatic. A CB enables its owner to become a member of a national party line whose main purpose is to transmit and receive gossip. Granted, the gossip is broadly based and covers a wide spectrum of areas concerning travel, but when important issues of road conditions, Smokey reports, and emergency calls are removed, the remainder of the dialogue is small talk.

Truckers were the first "Good Buddies." *Courtesy Marsha Holmberg.*

When the CB craze hit middle America, most new buyers had little knowledge of the unique dialogue that filtered over the airwaves. First-time users were easily detected when they used little known police 10-signals to ask a question or request a radio check. The old hands had developed a disc-jockey type jargon that was a mixture of truckers' occupational slang, folklore borrowed from similar occupations, and variations of folk sayings of Arkie-Okies.[5] Some regions have special jargon, but by the nature of the interstate trucking industry any new phrase is rapidly spread from coast to coast. Truckers from Washington to Florida use the nasal twang of West Texas bull haulers and broadcast the latest fashionable phrase.

Simultaneously the language erased regional differences and created a class bias. From its early inception until the present, channel 19 has been the trucker's domain. When less than a million sets were on the market, everyone used 19, and, when too many tried to speak on the channel, the sender would request that the receiver go to another channel where they could communicate. Truckers were happy to interrupt their lonely journey to talk to another "good buddy." The airwaves were friendly, and many social commentators as well as CB users were forecasting a nationwide brotherhood—a middle-class humanitarian movement.

The first few years of CB popularity, after the trucker strike, appeared to fulfill the forecast of such a movement. The mass media finally had found a cultural phenomenon that was of interest to all socioeconomic and ethnic groups in America. "Good Buddies" reported accidents, brought criminals to justice, saved lives, carried gas to stranded motorists, delivered babies, found lost children and sick dogs, spotted tornados, and became tour guides. All CBers became part of the good buddy generation and each became a member of a national folk cult with the purchase of a small electronic gadget. Not only did mass media report on newsworthy items that the CB was involved in, but also magazines devoted to this greatly expanding segment of the population gushed forth. Thus, with the abundance of newspaper coverage and television reporting, coupled with the public's desire to become part of this brotherhood of travelers, the CB became more than a form of communications. It became a way of life.

A large segment of the Good Buddy generation transmitting on major highways are involved in giving Smokey reports. Among these Smokey spotters a high percentage are hedging on the 55 mile per hour speed limit, commonly referred to as the "double nickel." The ideal, and often mythical, situation is to form a convoy. The point, or front door, of the convoy, often changing about twice per hour, warns those behind him if a Smokey is ahead. The last vehicle in the line, identified as the back door, shares the same responsibility for the opposite direction. Most often the report of a state trooper's location is recorded by mile markers, and, if he is "taking pictures and giving out green stamps," drivers thereby are warned that a radar unit is working and tickets are being issued.

When enough traffic is present to give sufficient Smokey warnings, a motorist can learn of impending danger several miles in each direction. However, in many states highway patrolmen monitor CB channels to make certain that any emergency calls are answered. Some states allow their troopers to transmit, but in most states they can only monitor the emergency channel. Part of the CB folklore, which has some elements of truth, has Smokey utilizing the CB to give the all-clear signal and then arresting the speeder as he comes over the next hill. The popular song, "White Knight," uses this often-repeated story as its central theme.

The rise in CB usage for other illegal activities concerns law enforcement much more than the evasion of speed laws. Truckers are able to avoid weigh stations by taking back roads or by waiting until the word is passed that the station has closed. Hot loads, either over-weighted trailers or illegal cargo, can escape detection by the driver monitoring the airwaves. Moreover, some motorists who call for help are robbed, and often truckers who ask for directions in a strange town are lured to a deserted part of town to be hijacked.

Ladies of the evening, aware of the large and receptive audience tuning in to the CB, advertise their wares from mobile homes. Police attempt to arrest many of the "hookers of the airwaves" but like their counterparts who walk the street, their fines are usually small, and they are plying their trade the following day on another part of the interstate. Some humorous stories have come from the soiled doves of the turnpike. One trooper in Pennsylvania, explaining his latest case involving soliciting sexual favors over the CB, told of long weeks trying to find a hooker who used the handle, "Shrimp Cocktail." When the troopers finally broke into her camper-van to arrest her, they were surprised to find she was a midget. Another similar incident occurred on Interstate 40 approximately 100 miles west of Oklahoma City. State troopers were asked by local citizens to arrest a highway hooker that worked the area. Rumors had circulated that she had a wooden leg, but the troopers laughed at the idea. However, when she was apprehended, not only did she have a wooden leg, but also she was the local sheriff's daughter.[6]

"The Iowa Gear Jammer" and his co-driving wife. *Courtesy Marsha Holmberg.*

Much of the attraction of the CB is that the sender is able to remain anonymous. Instead of using their given names, or in the case of ham radio operators call numbers, CBers give their handles. It is difficult to make any generalizations about the selection of a handle, but they seem to fall in several categories. Often husband and wife will choose names that describe them as a couple. "Tinbender" and his wife, "Lady Tinbender," probably have had a few accidents. "Ever Ready" and "Never Ready" would indicate that at least one couple in America still believes that the male sex drive is often blunted with a female headache.

Some handles reflect occupations: "Pig Jockey" hauls logs to market; "Paperhanger" makes a living installing wallpaper; and "Wire Nut" works for the telephone company. Other handles, such as "5-iron," "Old Prospector," or "Bear Tracker," symbolize hobbies. However, the most colorful of the CB handles are those that reflect personality traits. "Rainbow," "Moonbeam," "Moondust," or "Sunshine" conjure up an entirely different image of a female than does "Scarlet Letter," "Sensuous Woman," "Midnight Queen," or "Slinkey." Just as many women want to appear pure or sexy, so men often opt for macho-sounding handles. "Wild Bill," "Rattlesnake," "Mule Skinner," "Screaming Eagle," or "Texas Beaver Stretcher" would be the handles you would expect would be used to answer the feminine voice who identified herself as the "Silver Beaver."[7]

Handles not only provide an opportunity for CBers to assign a name to themselves, identifying those personality characteristics which are most important to them, but also senders have a large, sometimes captive, audience that they do not have to meet face-to-face. This allows CB-users a communication outlet that is not provided in other social settings—to speak freely without fear of social restraint. Thus the CB is often considered part of the communications frontier—a technological display of western egalitarianism.

This equality, or absence of social elitism, occurred when there were few CB's operating. However, with the explosion of CB purchasing, each of the 23 channels attracted a different socioeconomic, occupational, educational or ethnic class. Truckers controlled channel 19, and channel 9 remained for emergencies, but the rest of the channels were dominated by different groups according to geographical region. In areas where a heavy concentration of ethnic groups live, they manage to dominate several channels. In some areas where ethnic groups have a strong sense of cultural heritage, the native tongue is used over the airwaves. This same, self-imposed isolation separates teenagers, CB clubs, and even the counter-culture generation.

Some members of channels have coffee breaks, beer parties, or other forms of social gatherings. Moreover, members of the well-established channels have base stations, ranging from very exotic and expensive equipment to portable units that are removed from their vehicles and used at work or at home. Within the pecking order of channel groupies, one or two of the base stations monitor the channel and assume the role of switchboard operator. This role as "channel mother" is full-time.

Often CBers spend 20 hours per day on the air. In some cases shut-in, retired, or unemployed good buddies are responsible for directing the channel. With the use of more powerful transmitters than are allowed by FCC regulations, base stations can "shut down" (block out) most conversations on any given channel. Therefore if the base operation wants to talk, he talks "over" other transmissions. If a dialogue is not to his pleasing, or if the sender is not part of his group, or in some cases if the sender is using vile language, the base station "keys in" and blocks all signals on the channel.

Signal boosting by the use of linear power transformers is not confined to operators of base stations. Many mobile units use power assisting equipment to "run skip." With this extra and illegal power, the CB's range is increased from a few miles to hundreds and when the conditions are perfect, transmissions can cross the nation. Not only do these illegal operators dominate the channel they are sending on but also "bleed over" and block several channels on either side. The understaffed FCC fines a small percentage of those engaged in such illegal activities, but most can transmit for months without fear of being caught.

Within the last few years most travelers have turned off their sets when close to metropolitan areas, for the airwaves are too congested. Often the only clear transmissions that are heard are those coming from linear sets. Moreover, many CBers have developed social, cultural, and class biases and stereotyped other good buddies. These prejudices follow traditional socioeconomic and racial patterns, but a new dimension has been added— occupational bias. Truckers have recently closed ranks, rarely conversing over the CB with anyone that is not a member of their occupation.

With this resistance by the leaders of the good buddy generation, the intrusion of the general public into their private domain has decreased—the faddism of the CB has faded. After hours of listening to worn-out phrases and constant static, travelers have found more pleasure in turning off their sets. Moreover, reporting the whereabouts of Smokey is becoming less popular with CBers, for the system fails to protect the speeder from receiving tickets. Most have surrendered in the war against the federally imposed speed limit. Now channels mark social divisions, and the gap between channel 19 and other channels continues to grow. The truckers' folklore is still being broadcast over many of the channels, but verbal access to this modern-day folk hero is becoming more difficult with each passing year.

Conclusion

Historically, Americans have held tightly to folk tales, myths, and legends, and most often these stories and beliefs have been passed from generation to generation. The working man has been the most popular folk hero, for he was engaged in romantic occupations, displayed rugged individualism, fought against great odds and won, and had a freedom of mobility that Americans long for. However, during the last 50 years, most of these heroes have vanished, machines have taken their jobs, and the electronic, mass media has replaced folktales. Where fifty years ago the family was entertained during the evening hours by folktales, anecdotes, and yarns spun by the older generation, television now dominates the living room. The electronic intrusion has not stopped with the living room; with the invention of transistors, mini-transistors, and silicone wafers, verbal communication in almost any social setting can be avoided.

Moreover, in the massive movement of population from rural, agricultural regions to urban, industrial centers, much of the basic cultural heritage was lost. Oral folktales that enlightened the younger generation on the farm had little meaning to urban youth. Occupational heroes were replaced with media heroes, and with the changing mood of the nation's youth, heroes rose and fell. These new stars from television, movies, and the recording industry were products to be sold until the public's demand was satisfied. Seldom did the modern hero possess more than a one-dimensional character, and he offered little cultural or social heritage to pass on to the next generation. Thus, in such a complex society, folk heroes have little time to develop, for mass media dispels any myths before they can become part of the folk tradition. Moreover, what mythical heroes that have managed to survive through folktales have been exposed by accurate media reporting.

Modern-day man, faced with problems of a rapidly changing world, was left without a working hero. Traditional heroes were able to do the work of 10 men, banish the villain, and save the virgin. But the battlefield had shifted from the open range, the mining camp, and the timber stands, and the enemy was not a stampeding herd, a mine cave-in, or a log jam. The villain was complexity—big business, big government, and big debts. Crime rates soared, the counter culture revolted, and the computer appeared to be on its way to controlling America—the silent majority was finally labeled.

The longing for the "good old days" became infectious with the oil embargo, for many experts were predicting a national disaster—a devastating energy crisis. With the exception of wartime conditions, Americans were not accustomed to shortages of any kind, and cheap and abundant energy was part of the American tradition. Rumors and charges spread that oil companies had conspired to create a false shortage in order to raise prices. Other stories helped strengthen this conspiracy theory: about a glass carburetor that supposedly was invented by a small-town mechanic, which allowed an automobile to travel 60 miles on one gallon of gasoline, and which was purchased by a major oil company for millions of dollars and taken off the market. Another story tells of a customer who comments to an automobile dealer that he has been getting 100 miles per gallon in his new car. After the car is serviced, the experimental carburetor that mistakenly had been put on an average production car was replaced with a normal gas guzzling variety.

The feeling of helplessness and frustration, accented with outbreaks of anger, had little impact on the crisis. Only with the trucker strike did the common man have a spokesman—the independent trucker—championing his cause. Drivers banded together in loose confederations without electing leaders, without paying dues, and without the help of big labor, big government, or big corporations. Truckers blocked interstates with their rigs, committed acts of violence, and broke governmental regulations to fight against a complex escalation of fuel prices. Symbolically, the public saw this as the struggle of a disappearing breed of men—the last American cowboy—trying to save his occupation.

Media coverage did little to dispel the public's notion of the independent trucker's image. Moreover, truckers attempted to live up to this image of the last hurrah for the working man. Madison Avenue was able to capitalize on the trucker image with country and western songs, a few grade "B" movies, television shows, T-shirts with "Keep on Trucking" printed across the front, and millions of CB sets. However, the trucker had more staying power than other media heroes because they were not slick nor were they represented by one character. They were struggling each day, much like the common man, trying to salvage their way of life. Like most heroes, however, this once proud, independent, masculine folk hero fell under close public scrutiny, and, as with other folk heroes of the past, may soon disappear—destroyed by reality.

At first, truckers liked the national attention given their occupation, but soon every "mother's son" was trying to talk to these once-silent heroes. The private domain of the open road was overrun with the constant chatter of pseudo-truckers. And, much like the cowboy's lament of 100 years earlier, owner-operators needed more elbow room. Yet this time it was not the open range but the airwaves that experienced a population explosion. This shift in attitude of the trucker could come from the failure of the truckers' strike to produce any significant returns. Instead of fuel price reduction, the cost of diesel fuel continued to rise, and speed limits not only stayed at 55 miles per hour but also were being enforced. As all overhead costs continued to soar and freight rates remained constant, truckers were forced to drive more hours to maintain the same income.

This loss in revenue forced many owner-operators to sell their rigs or to lease them to major freighting companies. In addition to the obvious loss in status suffered by the independent trucker, he also pays a higher psychological cost. Governmental regulations and regulators are becoming more numerous, and in many states the letter of the law is being applied. Interstate truckers report that the state of Pennsylvania will take drivers to jail for a few miles per hour infraction of posted speed limits. Fines of $200 are not uncommon for late log entries in Kansas, and the list continues to grow each day. Interstate truckers with bloodshot eyes or day-old beards are likely candidates to be checked at weigh stations by Department of Transportation officials or highway patrolmen for faulty logs. Therefore drivers use Visine and portable electric razors before entering weigh stations.

Owner-operators, without sufficient cash flow for a downpayment on a new rig, can enter into an economic arrangement with a freighting company. They lose the freedom of sole ownership but maintain partial control of their own destiny. A standard agreement between freighting firms and independents provides that the trucker is advanced the downpayment for a new rig, but he must lease his new tractor to the lender and pay a percentage of his gross revenues to the firm in repayment of the loan. Thus on a round trip from New York to California the owner-operator will receive 70 percent of the gross revenue and the firm which owns the certified route will receive 30 percent. The trucker provides labor, fuel, and maintenance, and the firm provides the freighting contract and the permit.

Out of his gross income, the trucker has to pay his co-driver, his bank payment, and part of the freighting firm's advance for his downpayment. Thus freighting firms avoid the high overhead cost of operating their own trucks and many of the problems of employee-management relationships. By the same token, the trucker struggles to make his payments, and often, after a hard week of driving round trip from coast to coast, he breaks even. To improve his economic condition, the independent trucker must avoid governmental regulations. Instead of hiring a co-driver and driving the maximum number of hours allowed by law, a ghost driver is created. Logs are filled out in order to satisfy the Department of Transportation officials, and he is paid in cash to reduce Internal Revenue's suspicions. Truckers also haul freight for less than the rate schedules' minimum and receive unreported cash, avoiding hours of paperwork and taxes which might make the difference between profit and loss.

Husband-and-wife team, Sonny "Jailbird" and Tammy "Cricket" Camden, enjoy working together. *From the author's collection.*

The new American cowboy enjoys reading mythical accounts of the first cowboys. *From the author's collection.*

The high economic and psychological cost paid daily by independent truckers has resulted in a basic distrust and contempt for those outside their profession. Union and company drivers are often looked on with the same disdain as four wheelers or governmental representatives. The challenge for today's owner-operator is not to transverse the nation in record time but rather to stay in business. From this constant struggle to make payments and to avoid governmental regulations, drivers have become hostile to any outside interference in their day-to-day routine. The optimism that created the feeling of brotherhood which existed during the trucker slowdown and strike has now turned to pessimism. Not only are high fuel prices and 55 mile-per-hour speed limits and low profits still plaguing the trucker, but also governmental legislation has been introduced in Congress to limit driving time to eight hours per day. Moreover, reflecting the trend among other blue-collar workers, wives are now forced into the market place in order to supplement the family income.

During the last few years, husband and wife teams have almost become an economic necessity for many independent truckers trying to remain solvent. And, like the cowboy in countless western novels, wives are symbolic of the taming of a restless western spirit. The heroic frontier is rapidly fading from the interstate. The trucker will never regain the freedom or the folk image he had before the oil embargo. With increasing overhead costs, regulations, and energy shortages, the owner-operator will pass by the wayside much like general stores, soda fountains, and shoeshine parlors. Possibly, historians and folklorists during the next century will single out the 1970s as the "Golden Age of the Trucker," and hundreds of pulp accounts will relate the exciting stories of independent truckers evading speed traps, taking back roads with hot loads, and riding off into the sunset behind the wheel of their Peterbilt in the company of an attractive female hitchhiker dressed only in a raincoat.

NOTES

CHAPTER 1

[1]Most of the data in this chapter was garnered from 78 interviews with truckers at truckstops located along Interstate 35 and Interstate 40.

[2]See "Strip Teases Featured at Truck Stop," *The Wichita Eagle and Beacon*, December 14, 1975, 5 D; Jane Stern, *Trucker: A Portrait of the Last American Cowboy* (New York: McGraw-Hill Book Co., 1975), 1-2; Fred E. H. Schroeder, "A Bellyful of Coffee," *Journal of Popular Culture*, II, No. 2 (Spring, 1967), 679-686.

[3]State Highway Patrolmen often play "White Knight" on the jukebox in response to truckers who play the song "Convoy."

CHAPTER 2

[1]Stuart Daggett, *Principles of Inland Transportation* (New York: Harper and Brothers, 1934), 128-130.

[2]John B. Rae, *The American Automobile* (Chicago: University of Chicago Press, 1965), 7.

[3]*Ibid.*, 8-11.

[4]*Ibid.*, 13-15.

[5]*Ibid.*, 32.

[6]Archer Butler Hulbert, *The Future of Road-Making in America* (Cleveland: Arthur H. Clark Co., 1905), 80.

[7]Ray Giles, "The Industrial Motor Car," *Colliers' Automobile Supplement*, XLVII: No. 16 (January 6, 1912), 13.

[8]Robert F. Karolevitz, *This Was Trucking, A Pictorial History of the First Quarter Century of Commercial Motor Vehicles* (Seattle: Superior Publishing Co., 1966), 35-39.

[9]*Ibid.*

[10]*Ibid.*

[11]Theodore M. L. Von Keler, "The Farmer and the Motor Car," *Colliers' Automobile Supplement,* L, No. 3 (January 9, 1913), 36.

[12]Rollin W. Hutchinson, Jr., "The Wastrel Horse," *Colliers' Automobile Supplement,* XLV, No. 17 (January 9, 1915), 21.

[13]"Motor-Trucks and Motor Cars," *The Literary Digest,* XLVI, No. 8 (February 22, 1913), 405.

[14]Edward Mott Woolley, "Motordom Mobilized," *Colliers,* LX, No. 16 (December 29, 1917), 7.

[15]Hutchinson, "The Wastrel Horse," *Colliers',* 21.

[16]Rollin W. Hutchinson, Jr., "Motor Trucks-The New Freighters," *Worlds' Work,* XXIII, No. 3 (January, 1912), 269.

[17]Herbert Casson, Rollin W. Hutchinson, Jr., and L. W. Ellis, *Horse, Truck, and Tractor* (Chicago: F. G. Browne Co., 1913), 22-23.

[18]Hutchinson, "Motor Truck-The New Freighters," *World's Work,* 268.

[19]*Ibid.*

[20]Hutchinson, "The Wastrel Horse," *Colliers',* 21.

[21]Hutchinson, "Motor Trucks-The New Freighters," *World's Work,* 270-271.

[22]"The Nation's Industrial Progress," *The Outlook,* XXVI, No. 3 (April 3, 1918), 546.

[23]Hutchinson, "The Wastrel Horse," *Colliers',* 21.

[24]Karolevitz, *This Was Trucking,* 56-61.

[25]*Ibid.*

[26]*Ibid.*

[27]*Ibid.*

[28]Rollin W. Hutchinson, Jr., "The Motor Truck in Peace and War," *Colliers' Automobile Supplement,* LVI, No. 17 (January 8, 1916), 51.

[29]*Ibid.*

[30]*Ibid.,* 48.

[31]"The Nation's Industrial Progress," *The Outlook,* XXVI, No. 3 (October 16, 1918), 663; see also, The White Company, *White Trucks in Military Service* (Cleveland: The White Company, 1918), 7.

[32]*House Doc.,* Doc. No. 503, Sixty-fifth Congress, 2nd Session, Vol. V, 3.

[33]George Chatburn, *Highways and Highway Transportation* (New York: Thomas Y. Crowell Co., 1923), 137.

[34]Hutchinson, "The Motor Truck in Peace and War," *Colliers',* 51.

[35]*Ibid.*

[36]Motor Vehicle Manufacturers Association of the United States, Inc., *Automobiles of America: Milestones, Pioneers, Roll Call, Highlights* (Detroit: Wayne State University Press, 1974), 283.

[37]John B. Rae, *The Road and the Car in American Life* (Cambridge, Mass.: The

M.I.T. Press, 1971), 128; Von Keler, "The Farmer and the Motor Car," *Colliers'*, 22-25.

[38]Rollin W. Hutchinson, Jr., "Motorized Highway Commerce," *Scribner's Magazine*, LV, No. 2 (February, 1914), 81.

[39]John Robinson, *Highways and Our Environment* (New York: McGraw-Hill Book Co., 1971), 36.

[40]*Ibid.*

[41]Chatburn, *Highways and Highway Transportation*, 140-141.

[42]F. L. Paxon, "The Highway Movement, 1916-1935," *American Historical Review*, LI, No. 2 (January, 1946), 250.

[43]Von Keler, "The Farmer and the Motor Car," *Colliers'*, 34.

[44]Hutchinson, "The Motor Truck in Peace and War," *Colliers'*, 53.

[45]C. D. Kinsman, *An Appraisal of Power on Farms in the United States*, U.S. Department of Agriculture Bulletin No. 1348, 1925, 71.

[46]Von Keler, "The Farmer and the Motor Car," *Colliers'*, 34.

[47]L. I. Hewes, "Roads Worth $35,000,000 a Year," *World's Work*, XXVI, No. 6 (October, 1912), 688-697.

[48]Hutchinson, "The Motor Truck in Peace and War," *Colliers'*, 53.

[49]J. K. Allen and Richard McElyea, *Impact of Improved Highways on the Economy of the United States* (Washington: Bureau of Public Roads, 1958), 179.

[50]Von Keler, "The Farmer and the Motor Car," *Colliers'*, 34.

[51]The Department of Agriculture, *Year Book, 1900* (Washington: Government Printing Office, 1901), 8.

[52]Chatburn, *Highways and Highway Transportation*, 137.

[53]*Ibid.*

[54]Von Keler, "The Farmer and the Motor Car," *Colliers'*, 34.

[55]Val Hart, *The Story of American Roads* (New York: William Sloane Associates, Inc., 1950), 188.

[56]Karolevitz, *This Was Trucking*, 43.

[57]*Ibid.*, 43-46.

[58]*Ibid.*

CHAPTER 3

[1]Henry B. Joy, "Transcontinental Trails," *Scribner's Magazine*, LV, No. 2 (February, 1914), 161.

[2]*Report of the New Jersey Commission of Public Roads, 1900*, 81.

[3]Ewing Galloway, "The Way to Good Roads," *Collier's Automobile Section*, LII, No. 1 (January 10, 1914), 5-6.

[4]Department of Commerce, Bureau of Public Roads, *Highway Statistics Summary of 1955*, tables HF-120, HF-200.

[5]*Congressional Record*, Vol. XXIV, January 26, 1893, 883.

[6]*Report of the Secretary of Agriculture, 1893* (Washington: Government Printing Office, 1894), 36.

[7]Department of Agriculture, *Office of Road Inquiry,* Bulletin No. 1 (Washington: Government Printing Office, 1893), 5.

[8]*Ibid.,* 5-7.

[9]Office of the Public Roads, *Federal Road Act, Regulations for Carrying Out,* Circular No. 65 (Washington: Government Printing Office, 1916).

[10]George M. Smerk, *Urban Transportation: The Federal Role* (Bloomington, Indiana: Indiana University Press, 1965), 121.

[11]*Ibid.,* 121-122.

[12]*Ibid.*

[13]*House Report,* Report No. 451. Sixty-seventh Congress, 1st Session, Vol. XXI, 1-11.

[14]*Ibid.*

[15]*Ibid.*

[16]U.S. Department of Commerce, Bureau of Public Roads, *Highway Statistics: Summary to 1945* (Washington: U.S. Government Printing Office, 1947).

[17]*Ibid.,* Frank H. Mossman and Newton Morton, *Principles of Transportation* (New York: The Ronald Press, 1957), 406-411.

[18]Charles Luna, *The UTU Handbook of Transportation* (New York: Popular History, 1971), 214-215; *Highways Development, Use, Financing* (Washington: Association of American Railroads, 1955), 10.

CHAPTER 4

[1]Rollin W. Hutchinson, Jr., "Motor Trucks-The New Freighters," *World's Work,* XXIII, No. 3 (January, 1912), 270.

[2]David B. Harrison, "The Akron-Boston Express of 1917," *Car Classics,* Editions of the American Automobile Association, 1966, 11.

[3]*Goodyear Tire News* (September, 1917), 1.

[4]Harrison, "The Akron-Boston Express of 1917," 11-14.

[5]*Ibid.*

[6]*Ibid.*

[7]*Ibid.*

[8]*Ibid.*

[9]Robert F. Karolevitz, *This Was Trucking* (Seattle: Superior Publishing Co., 1966), 62.

[10]*Ibid.,* 61-63.

[11]Edward Mott Woolley, "Motordom Mobilized," *Colliers',* LX, No. 16 (December 29, 1917), 9.

[12]Walter Tips, "Vignette: September-1918, Texas Trucks in the Rainbow," *Military History of Texas and the Southwest,* Vol. XII, No. 1, 8-13.

[13]*Ibid.*

[14]G. A. Kissell, "Motor Trucks on America's Bread Line," *The Outlook,* XXVI, No. 5 (July 3, 1918), 394-395.

[15]Alfred Lief, *The Firestone Story* (New York: McGraw-Hill, 1951), pp. 99-119.

[16]*Ibid.*, 120.

[17]Motor Vehicle Manufacturer's Association of the United States, Inc., *Automobiles of America: Milestones, Pioneers, Roll Call, Highlights* (Detroit: Wayne State University Press, 1974), 283.

[18]Board of Investigation and Research, *Technological Trends in Transportation* (Washington: U.S. Government Printing Office, 1945), 45.

[19]Lief, *The Firestone Story,* 138-139.

[20]*Technological Trends in Transportation,* 45.

[21]Board of Investigation and Research, *Technological Trends in Transportation* (Washington: U.S. Government Printing Office, 1945), 48.

[22]Motor Vehicle Manufacturer's Association of the United States, Inc., *Automobiles of America: Milestones, Pioneers, Roll Call, Highlights* (Detroit: Wayne State University Press, 1974), 283.

[23]*Technological Trends in Transportation,* 48-51.

[24]*Ibid.*

[25]*Ibid.*

[26]P. J. Russell, *The Motor Wagons* (Akron: The Pioneer Motor Traffic Club of Akron, 1971), 62-67.

[27]*Ibid.*, 67.

[28]Athel F. Denham, *20 Years' Progress in Commercial Motor Vehicles* (Washington: Automobile Council for War Production, 1942), 164.

[29]*Ibid.*, 171-172.

[30]*Ibid.*, 169-173.

[31]Denham, *20 Years' Progress in Commercial Motor Vehicles,* 178-179.

[32]*Automobiles of America,* 40-41.

[33]Denham, *20 Years' Progress in Commercial Motor Vehicles,* 128.

[34]*Ibid.*, 97.

[35]*Automobiles of America,* 23.

[36]*Ibid.*, 33.

[37]Commercial Car Journal, 50th Anniversary Special, *The Golden Years of Highway Transportation* (Philadelphia: Chiton Publication, 1961), 88.

[38]*Technological Trends in Transportation,* 60.

[39]*Ibid.*, 59.

[40]*Ibid.*, 58.

[41]*Motor Truck Facts, 1973* (New York: Motor Vehicle Manufacturers Association of the United States, 1974), 15.

CHAPTER 5

[1]Department of Commerce, Bureau of Public Roads, *Impact of Improved Highways on the Economy of the United States* (Washington: U.S. Government Printing Office, 1958), 178-181; Interview with Robert J. Brassfield, Veterans' Administration Employment Service, Wichita, Kansas, August 27, 1975; Robert

Leiter, *The Teamsters' Union: A Study of its Impact* (New York: Bookman Associates, Inc., 1957), 138.

[2]John Montville, "Wheels for Commerce, A History of American Motor Trucks," *The American Car Since 1775* (New York: The Automobile Quarterly, 1965), 400.

[3]Federal Coordinator of Transportation, *Hours, Wages, and Working Conditions in the Intercity Motor Transportation Industries* (Washington: U.S. Government Printing Office, 1936), 57.

[4]*Ibid.*, 69.

[5]*Ibid.*, 119.

[6]*Ibid.*, 99.

[7]*Ibid.*, 86-87.

[8]*Ibid.*, 91-93.

[9]*Ibid.*

[10]*Ibid.*, 99.

[11]*Ibid.*

[12]*Ibid.*, 116.

[13]*Ibid.*, 117.

[15]James C. Johnson, *Trucking Mergers; A Regulatory Viewpoint* (Lexington, Massachusetts: D. C. Heathand Company, 1973), 3.

[16]"Doing it the Hard Way," *Forbes* (December 1, 1975), 21-23.

[17]"Resume of Growth," *Lee Way Motor Freight* (August 1, 1977), 2.

[18]Interview, Hugh Thomas, January 12, 1976.

[19]Susan Sheehan, "On the Road With a Bedbug Hauler," *New York Times Magazine* (November 12, 1972), 36.

[20]Robert C. Fellmeth, *The Interstate Commerce Omission* (New York: Grossman Publishers, 1970), 226-239.

[21]*Ibid.*

[22]Don Pearce, "Those Truck Driving Men," *Esquire*, LXXVIII, No. 6 (December, 1972), 328.

[23]Fellmeth, *The Interstate Commerce Omission*, 230-235.

[24]*Ibid.*

[25]*Ibid.*, 236-237.

[26]Interview, "Tex," December 2, 1975.

[27]P. J. Russell, *The Motor Wagons* (Akron: The Pioneer Motor Traffic Club of Akron, 1971), 131, 268.

[28]Interview, "Tex," December 2, 1975.

CHAPTER 6

[1]*House Doc.*, Doc. No. 408, Sixty-seventh Congress, 1st Session, Vol. VII, 348-365.

[2]*Ibid.*

[3]*Senate Doc.*, Doc. No. 1734, Sixty-first Congress, 1st Session, Vol. XI, 402.

[4]*Motor Bus and Truck Operation,* 140 I.C.C. 685.

[5]*Coordination of Motor Transportation,* 182 I.C.C. 263.

[6]John R. Meyer, Merton J. Peck, John Stenason and Charles Zwich, *The Economics of Competition in the Transportation Industries* (Cambridge, Mass.: Harvard University Press, 1964), 215-217.

[7]195 I.C.C. 5, 45, p. 377.

[8]*Ibid.,* 376.

[9]*Ibid.,* 376.

[10]*Historical Development of Transport Coordination and Integration in the United States* (Washington: U.S. Government Printing Office, 1950), 92-101; see also Frank H. Mossman and Newton Morton, *Principles of Transportation* (New York: The Ronald Press, 1957), 80-96.

[11]*Rock Island Motor Transit Company* vs. *United States,* 55 M.C.C. 567.

[12]*Motor Bus and Truck Operation,* 140 I.C.C. 685.

[13]*Ibid.*

[14]John R. Meyer, Merton J. Peck, John Stenason, and Charles Zwick, *The Economics of Competition in the Transportation Industries* (Cambridge, Mass.: Harvard University Press, 1964), 10-14.

[15]James C. Nelson, "The Effects of Entry Control in Surface Transport," James C. Nelson, et al., *Transportation Economics* (New York: Bureau of Economic Research, 1965), 413.

[16]Walter Adams and James Hendry, *Trucking, Mergers, Concentration and Small Business: An Analysis of Interstate Commerce Commission Policy, 1950-1956* (Washington: U.S. Government Printing Office, 1957), 32.

[17]Robert C. Fellmeth, *The Interstate Commerce Omission* (New York: Grossman Publishers, 1970), 136-141.

[18]Walter Adams, "The Role of Competition in the Regulated Industries," *American Economic Review,* XLVII, No. 2 (May, 1958), 533.

[19]*Traffic World* (January 28, 1956), 21.

[20]Association of American Railroads, *Highway Motor Transportation: Report of Subcommittee on Motor Transport of the Railroad for the Study of Transportation* (Washington: Association of American Railroads, 1945), 101.

[21]Bureau of Public Roads, *Highways and Economics and Social Changes* (Washington: U.S. Government Printing Office, 1964), 58.

CHAPTER 7

[1]Wendell Rawls, Jr., "Strip Teases Featured at Truck Stop," *The Wichita Eagle and Beacon,* December 14, 1975, 5D.

[2]Public Health Bulletin No. 265, *Fatigue and Hours of Service of Interstate Truck Drivers* (Washington: U.S. Government Printing Office, 1941), 101.

[3]Jane Stern, *Trucker, A Portrait of the Last American Cowboy* (New York: McGraw-Hill, 1975), 98.

[4]*Ibid.*

[5]Richard Symanski, "Prostitution in Nevada," *Annals of the Association of American Geographers,* LXIV, No. 3 (September, 1974), 373.

[6]Stern, *Truckers,* 116.

[7]Rawls, "Strip Teases Featured at Truck Stop," 5D.

[8]*Ibid.*

[9]Interview, Don Mann, Salesman, Kenworth Co., Oklahoma City, Oklahoma, March 17, 1976.

[10]The Kenworth Truck Company dealership in Oklahoma City, Oklahoma, in 1975, sold the top-of-the-line trucks for an average price of $45,000. However, one truck was ordered in March of 1976 that cost the customer $52,000.

[11]Advertisement Pamphlet, *W-900,* Kenworth Truck Company, 1974.

[12]*Ibid.*

[13]Advertisement Pamphlet, *Kenworth Paint Schemes,* Kenworth Truck Company.

[14]*Ibid.*

[15]*Ibid.*

[16]Advertisement Pamphlet, *The Kenworth W-900,* Kenworth Truck Company.

[17]Pamphlet, *W-900.*

[18]Interview, Don Mann.

[19]Advertisement Pamphlet, *V.I.T.* Kenworth Truck Company.

[20]Ross Farland, *Human Factors in Highway Safety* (Boston: Harvard School of Public Health, 1954), 39-45.

[21]C. W. McCall's recording "Convoy."

[22]Interview with "Tex," December 2, 1975. He was one of the many truckers who refused to give a Christian name.

[23]*Ibid.*

[24]McFarland, *Human Factors,* 125.

[25]*Ibid.,* p. 127; out of 78 interviews conducted by the author, all long-haul drivers had experienced hypnagogic phenomenon.

[26]Interview, George Blanton, December 1, 1975.

[27]McFarland, *Human Factors,* 126-127.

[28]Public Health Bulletin No. 265, *Fatigue and Hours of Service of Interstate Truck Drivers* (Washington: U.S. Government Printing Office, 1941), 100-101.

[29]Stern, *Trucker: A Portrait of the Last American Cowboy,* 127; see also, Donn Pearce, "Those Truck Driving Men," *Esquire,* LXXVII, No. 6 (December, 1972), 322.

[30]*Fatigue and Hours of Service,* 101.

[31]*Ibid.*

[32]Interview, Hugh Thomas, January 12, 1976.

[33]Pearce, "Those Truck Driving Men," 322.

CHAPTER 8

[1]David Hicks, Citizens Band Radio Handbook, (Indianapolis: Howard W. Sams Co., 1976), 7-10.

[2]"The New Highway" Guerrillas, *Time,* (December 17, 1973), 33.

[3]"House Votes Speed Limit of 55 M.P.H. for Nation," *New York Times,* (December 4, 1973), 1.

[4]John Thompson, *The Official CB Book,* (New York: Ballantine Books, 1976), 19.

[5]"Arkie-Okies" are most often identified as those residents of Texas, Arkansas, and Oklahoma that are from rural backgrounds and have a pronounced slang.

[6]The highway patrolman that related these anecdotes requested that their names not be used.

[7]A. E. Crawford, "The Phenomenon of the Citizens Band Radio; A CB Owners Survey" (unpublished manuscript), 24.

SELECTED BIBLIOGRAPHY

I. GOVERNMENT

Adams, Walter and James Hendry. *Trucking, Mergers, Concentration and Small Business: An Analysis of Interstate Commerce Commission Policy, 1950-1956*. Washington: U.S. Government Printing Office, 1957.

Allen, J. K. and Richard McElyea. *Impact of Improved Highways on the Economy of the United States*. Washington: Bureau of Public Roads, 1958.

Board of Investigation and Research. *Technological Trends in Transportation*. Washington: U.S. Government Printing Office, 1945.

Bureau of Public Roads. *Highways and Economics and Social Changes*. Washington: U.S. Government Printing Office, 1964.

————. *Highway Statistics: Summary of 1955*. Washington: U.S. Government Printing Office, 1956.

————. *Highway Statistics: Summary of 1945*. Washington: U.S. Government Printing Office, 1947.

————. *Impact of Improved Highways on the Economy of the United States*. Washington: U.S. Government Printing Office, 1958.

Coordination of Motor Transportation, 182 I.C.C. 263.

Denham, Athel F. *20 Years' Progress in Commercial Motor Vehicles*. Washington: Automobile Council for War Production, 1942.

Department of Agriculture. *Office of Road Inquiry* (Bulletin No. 1.). Washington: U.S. Government Printing Office, 1893.

————. *Fatigue and Hours of Service of Interstate Truck Drivers* (Public Health Bulletin No. 265). Washington: U.S. Government Printing Office, 1941.

Federal Coordinator of Transportation. *Hours, Wages, and Working Conditions in the Intercity Motor Transportation Industries*. Washington: U.S. Government Printing Office, 1936.

164

Historical Development of Transport Coordination and Integration in the United States. Washington: U.S. Government Printing Office, 1950.

House Doc. Doc. No. 503, Sixty-fifth Congress, 2nd Session.

House Doc. Doc. No. 408, Sixty-seventh Congress, 1st Session, Vol. VII.

House Report. Report No. 451. Sixty-seventh Congress, 1st Session, Vol. XXI.

Kinsman, C. D. *An Appraisal of Power on Farms in the United States.* Department of Agriculture Bulletin No. 1348, 1925.

Motor Bus and Truck Operation, 140 I.C.C. 685.

Office of the Public Roads. *Federal Road Act, Regulations for Carrying Out* (Circular No. 65). Washington: U.S. Government Printing Office, 1916.

Report of the Secretary of Agriculture, 1893. Washington: U.S. Government Printing Office, 1894.

Report of The New Jersey Commission of Public Roads, 1900.

Rock Island Motor Transit Company vs. *United States,* 55 M.C.C. 567.

Senate Doc. Doc. No. 1734, Sixty-first Congress, 1st Session, Vol. XI.

II. BOOKS

Association of American Railroads. *Highway Development, Use, Financing.* Washington: Association of American Railroads, 1955.

————. *Highway Motor Transportation: Report of Subcommittee on Motor Transport of the Railroad for the Study of Transportation.* Washington: Association of American Railroads, 1945.

Casson, Herbert, Rollin W. Hutchinson, Jr., and L. W. Ellis. *Horse, Truck, and Tractor.* Chicago: F. G. Browne Co., 1913.

Chatburn, George. *Highways and Highway Transportation.* New York: Thomas Y. Crowell Co., 1923.

Commercial Car Journal, 50th Anniversary Special. *The Golden Years of Highway Transportation.* Philadelphia: Chiton Publication, 1961.

Daggett, Stuart. *Principles of Inland Transportation.* New York: Harper and Row, 1934.

Fellmeth, Robert C. *The Interstate Commerce Omission.* New York: Grossman Publishers, 1970.

Hart, Val. *The Story of American Roads.* New York: William Sloane Associated, Inc., 1950.

Hulbert, Archer Butler. *The Future of Road-making in America.* Cleveland: Arthur H. Clark Co., 1905.

Karolevitz, Robert F. *This was Trucking, A Pictorial History of the First Quarter Century of Commercial Motor Vehicles.* Seattle: Superior Publishing Co., 1966.

Leiter, Robert. *The Teamsters' Union: A Study of its Impact.* New York: Bookman Associates, Inc., 1957.

Lief, Alfred. *The Firestone Story.* New York: McGraw-Hill, 1951.

Luna, Charles. *The Utu Handbook of Transportation.* New York: Popular History, 1971.

Meyer, John R., *et al. The Economics of Competition in the Transportation Industries.* Cambridge: Harvard University Press, 1964.

McFarland, Ross. *Human Factors in Highway Safety.* Boston: Harvard School of Public Health, 1954.

Mossman, Frank H. and Newton Morton. *Principles of Transportation.* New York: The Ronald Press, 1957.

Motor Truck Facts, 1973. New York: Motor Vehicle Manufacturers Association of the United States, 1974.

Motor Vehicle Manufacturers Association of the United States, Inc. *Automobiles of America: Milestones, Pioneers, Roll Call, Highlights.* Detroit: Wayne State University Press, 1974.

Rae, John B. *The American Automobile.* Chicago: University of Chicago Press, 1965.

Robinson, John. *Highways and Our Environment.* New York: McGraw-Hill Book Co., 1971.

Russell, P. J. *The Motor Wagons.* Akron: The Pioneer Motor Traffic Club of Akron, 1971.

Smerk, George M. *Urban Transportation: The Federal Role.* Bloomington, Indiana: Indiana University Press, 1965.

Stern, Jane. *Trucker: A Portrait of the Last American Cowboy.* New York: McGraw-Hill Book Co., 1975.

White Company. *White Trucks in Military Service.* Cleveland: The White Company, 1918.

III. ARTICLES

Adams, Walter. "The Role of Competition in the Regulated Industries." *American Economic Review,* XLVII, No. 2 (May, 1958), 527-561.

Galloway, Ewing. "The Way to Good Roads." *Collier's Automobile Section,* LII, No. 1 (January 10, 1914), 5-6.

Giles, Ray. "The Industrial Motor Car." *Collier's Automobile Supplement,* XLVII, No. 16 (January 6, 1912), 13-15.

Hewes, L. I. "Roads Worth $35,000,000 a Year." *World's Work,* XXVI, No. 6 (October, 1912), 688-698.

Hutchinson, Rollin W. "Motorized Highway Commerce." *Scribner's Magazine,* LV, No. 2 (February, 1914), 181-192.

———. "The Motor Truck in Peace and War." *Collier's Automobile Supplement,* LVI, No. 17 (January 8, 1916), 43-56.

———. "The Wastrel Horse." *Collier's Automobile Supplement,* LVI: No. 17 (January 9, 1915), 21-25.

———. "Motor Trucks—The New Freighters." *World's Work.* XXIII, No. 3 (January, 1912), 268-282.

Joy, Henry B. "Transcontinental Trails." *Scribner's Magazine,* LV, No. 2 (February, 1914), 160-180.

Kissell, G. A. "Motor Trucks on America's Bread Line." *The Outlook,* XXVI, No. 5 (July 3, 1918), 394-395.

"Motor-Trucks and Motor-Cars." *The Literary Digest,* XLVI, No. 8 (February 22, 1913), 405-408.

"The Nation's Industrial Progress." *The Outlook,* XXVI, No. 3 (April 3, 1918), 663-664.

Nelson, James C. "The Effects of Entry Control in Surface Transport. Nelson, James C., *et al. Transportation Economics,* 1965, 410-452.

Paxon, F. L. "The Highway Movement." *American Historical Review,* LI, No. 2 (January, 1946), 236-253.

Pearce, Donn. "Those Truck Driving Men." *Esquire,* LXXVII, No. 6 (December, 1972), 322-332.

Schroeder, Fred E. H. "A Bellyful of Coffee." *Journal of Popular Culture,* II, No. 2 (Spring, 1967), 69-79.

Sheehan, Susan. "On the Road with a Bedbug Hauler," *New York Times* Magazine, CXLII, No. 18 (November 12, 1972), 36-37, 74-75, 83, 85-87, 90, 95, 97, 101-102.

Symanski, Richard. "Prostitution in Nevada." *Annals of the Association of American Geographers,* LXIV, No. 3 (September, 1973), 357-377.

Tips, Walter. "Vignette: September-1918, Texas Trucks in the Rainbow." *Military History of Texas and the Southwest,* XII, No. 1, 8-13.

Von Keler, Theodore M. R. "The Farmer and the Motor Car." *Collier's Automobile Supplement,* L, No. 3 (January 9, 1913), 22-25.

Woolley, Edward Mott. "Motordom Mobilized." *Collier's,* LX, No. 16 (December 29, 1917), 7-9.

IV. NEWSPAPERS

"Strip Teases Featured at Truck Stop." *The Wichita Eagle and Beacon* (December 14, 1975).

INDEX